About Behaviorism

About Behaviorism

B. F. Skinner

ALFRED A. KNOPF: New York

1974

THIS IS A BORZOI BOOK
PUBLISHED BY ALFRED A. KNOPF, INC.

Library of Congress Cataloging in Publication Data:
Skinner, Burrhus Frederic, date.
About behaviorism.
Bibliography: p.
1. Behaviorism. I. Title.
BF199.S54   150'.19'434   73-20768
ISBN 0-394-49201-3
ISBN 0-394-31856-0

Manufactured in the United States of America

Published May 22, 1974
Second Printing Before Publication

To Ernest Vargas and Barry Buzan

Contents

About Behaviorism

Introduction

Behaviorism is not the science of human behavior, it is the philosophy of that science. Some of the questions it asks are these: Is such a science really possible? Can it account for every aspect of human behavior? What methods can it use? Are its laws as valid as those of physics and biology? Will it lead to a technology, and if so, what role will it play in human affairs? Particularly important is its bearing on earlier treatments of the same subject. Human behavior is the most familiar feature of the world in which people live, and more must have been said about it than about any other thing; how much of what has been said is worth saving?

Some of these questions will eventually be answered by the success or failure of scientific and technological enterprises, but current issues are raised, and provisional answers are needed now. A great many intelligent people believe that answers have already been found and that they are all unpromising. Here, for example, are some of the things

3

commonly said about behaviorism or the science of behavior. They are all, I believe, wrong.

1. It ignores consciousness, feelings, and states of mind.

2. It neglects innate endowment and argues that all behavior is acquired during the lifetime of the individual.

3. It formulates behavior simply as a set of responses to stimuli, thus representing a person as an automaton, robot, puppet, or machine.

4. It does not attempt to account for cognitive processes.

5. It has no place for intention or purpose.

6. It cannot explain creative achievements—in art, for example, or in music, literature, science, or mathematics.

7. It assigns no role to a self or sense of self.

8. It is necessarily superficial and cannot deal with the depths of the mind or personality.

9. It limits itself to the prediction and control of behavior and misses the essential nature or being of man.

10. It works with animals, particularly with white rats, but not with people, and its picture of human behavior is therefore confined to those features which human beings share with animals.

11. Its achievements under laboratory control cannot be duplicated in daily life, and what it has to say about human behavior in the world at large is therefore unsupported metascience.

12. It is oversimplified and naïve and its facts are either trivial or already well known.

13. It is scientistic rather than scientific. It merely emulates the sciences.

14. Its technological achievements could have come about through the use of common sense.

15. If its contentions are valid, they must apply to the behavioral scientist himself, and what he says is therefore only what he has been conditioned to say and cannot be true.

16. It dehumanizes man; it is reductionistic and destroys man *qua* man.

17. It is concerned only with general principles and therefore neglects the uniqueness of the individual.

18. It is necessarily antidemocratic because the relation between experimenter and subject is manipulative, and its results can therefore be used by dictators but not by men of good will.

19. It regards abstract ideas such as morality or justice as fictions.

20. It is indifferent to the warmth and richness of human life, and it is incompatible with the creation and enjoyment of art, music, and literature and with love for one's fellow men.

These contentions represent, I believe, an extraordinary misunderstanding of the achievements and significance of a scientific enterprise. How can it be explained? The early history of the movement may have caused trouble. The first explicit behaviorist was John B. Watson, who in 1913 issued a kind of manifesto called *Psychology as the Behaviorist Views It*. As the title shows, he was not proposing a new science but arguing that psychology should be redefined as the study of behavior. This may have been a strategic mistake. Most of the psychologists at the time believed they were studying mental processes in a mental world of consciousness, and they were naturally not inclined to agree with Watson. Early behaviorists wasted a good deal of time, and confused an important central issue, by attacking the introspective study of mental life.

Watson himself had made important observations of instinctive behavior and was, indeed, one of the first ethologists in the modern spirit, but he was greatly impressed by new evidence of what an organism could learn to do, and he made some rather extreme claims about the potential of a newborn human infant. He himself called them exaggerations, but they have been used to discredit him ever since. His new science was also, so to speak, born prematurely. Very few scientific facts about behavior—particularly human behavior—were available. A shortage of facts is always a problem in a new science, but in Watson's aggressive program in a field as vast as human behavior it was especially damaging. He needed more factual support than he could find, and it is not surprising that much of what he said seemed oversimplified and naïve.

Among the behavioral facts at hand were reflexes and conditioned reflexes, and Watson made the most of them, but the reflex suggested a push-pull type of causality not incompatible with the nineteenth-century conception of a machine. The same impression was given by the work of the Russian physiologist Pavlov, published at about the same time, and it was not corrected by the stimulus-response psychology which emerged during the next three or four decades.

Watson naturally emphasized the most reproducible results he could find, and most of them had been obtained from animals—the white rats of animal psychology and Pavlov's dogs. It seemed to be implied that human behavior had no distinguishing characteristics. And to bolster his claim that psychology was a science, and to fill out his textbook, he borrowed from anatomy and physiology, and Pavlov took the same line by insisting that his experiments on behavior were really "an investigation of the physiological activity of the cerebral cortex," although neither man could point to any direct observations of the nervous system which threw light on behavior. They were also forced into hasty interpretations of complex behavior, Watson arguing that thinking was merely subvocal speech and Pavlov that language was simply a "second signal system." Watson had little or nothing to say about intention or purpose or creativity. He emphasized the technological promise of a science of behavior, but his examples were not incompatible with a manipulative control.

More than sixty years have passed since Watson issued his manifesto, and a great deal has happened in that time. The scientific analysis of behavior has made dramatic progress, and the shortcomings in Watson's account are now, I believe, chiefly of historical interest. Nevertheless, criticism has not greatly changed. All the misunderstandings listed above are to be found in current publications by philosophers, theologians, social scientists, historians, men and women of letters, psychologists, and many others. The vagaries of the early history of the movement can hardly suffice as an explanation.

Some trouble no doubt arises from the fact that human behavior is a sensitive field. Much is at stake in the way in which we look at ourselves, and a behavioristic formulation certainly calls for some disturbing changes. Moreover, terms originating in earlier formulations are deeply imbedded in our language, and they have had a place in both technical and nontechnical literature for centuries. Nevertheless, it would be unfair to argue that the critic has not been able to free himself from these historical prejudices. There must be some other reason why behaviorism as the philosophy of a science of behavior is still so seriously misunderstood.

I believe the explanation is this: the science itself is misunderstood. There are many different kinds of behavioral science, and some of them, as I shall show later, formulate the field in ways which do not raise important behavioristic issues. The criticisms listed above are most effectively answered by a special discipline, which has come to be called the experimental analysis of behavior. The behavior of individual organisms is studied in carefully controlled environments, and the relation between behavior and environment then formulated. Unfortunately, very little is known about this analysis outside the field. Its most active investigators, and there are hundreds of them, seldom make any effort to explain themselves to nonspecialists. As a result, few people are familiar with the scientific underpinnings of what, I believe, is the most cogent statement of the behavioristic position.

The behaviorism I present in this book is the philosophy of this special version of a science of behavior. The reader should know that not all behaviorists will agree with everything I say. Watson spoke for "the behaviorist," and in his time he *was* the behaviorist, but no one can assume that mantle today. What follows is admittedly—and, as a behaviorist, I must say necessarily—a personal view. I believe, however, that it is a consistent and coherent account, which satisfactorily answers the criticisms listed above.

I also believe in its importance. The major problems facing the world today can be solved only if we improve our understanding of human behavior. Traditional views have been around for centuries, and I think it is fair to say that they have proved to be inadequate. They are largely responsible for the situation in which we now find ourselves. Behaviorism offers a promising alternative, and I have written this book in an effort to make its position clear.

1

The Causes of Behavior

Why do people behave as they do? It was probably first a practical question: How could a person anticipate and hence prepare for what another person would do? Later it would become practical in another sense: How could another person be induced to behave in a given way? Eventually it became a matter of understanding and explaining behavior. It could always be reduced to a question about causes.

We tend to say, often rashly, that if one thing follows another, it was probably caused by it—following the ancient principle of *post hoc, ergo propter hoc* (after this, therefore because of this). Of many examples to be found in the explanation of human behavior, one is especially important here. The person with whom we are most familiar is ourself; many of the things we observe just before we behave occur within our body, and it is easy to take them as the causes of our behavior. If we are asked why we have spoken sharply to a friend, we may reply, "Because I felt angry."

It is true that we felt angry before, or as, we spoke, and so we take our anger to be the cause of our remark. Asked why we are not eating our dinner, we may say, "Because I do not feel hungry." We often feel hungry when we eat and hence conclude that we eat because we feel hungry. Asked why we are going swimming, we may reply, "Because I feel like swimming." We seem to be saying, "When I have felt like this before, I have behaved in such and such a way." Feelings occur at just the right time to serve as causes of behavior, and they have been cited as such for centuries. We assume that other people feel as we feel when they behave as we behave.

But where are these feelings and states of mind? Of what stuff are they made? The traditional answer is that they are located in a world of nonphysical dimensions called the mind and that they are mental. But another question then arises: How can a mental event cause or be caused by a physical one? If we want to predict what a person will do, how can we discover the mental causes of his behavior, and how can we produce the feelings and states of mind which will induce him to behave in a given way? Suppose, for example, that we want to get a child to eat a nutritious but not very palatable food. We simply make sure that no other food is available, and eventually he eats. It appears that in depriving him of food (a physical event) we have made him feel hungry (a mental event), and that because he has felt hungry, he has eaten the nutritious food (a physical event). But how did the physical act of deprivation lead to the feeling of hunger, and how did the feeling move the muscles involved in ingestion? There are many other puzzling questions of this sort. What is to be done about them?

The commonest practice is, I think, simply to ignore them. It is possible to believe that behavior expresses feelings, to anticipate what a person will do by guessing or asking him how he feels, and to change the environment in the hope of changing feelings while paying little if any attention to theoretical problems. Those who are not quite comfortable about such a strategy sometimes take refuge in physiology. Mind, it is said, will eventually be found to have a physical basis. As one neurologist recently put it "Everyone now accepts the fact that the brain provides the physical basis of human thought." Freud believed that his very complicated mental apparatus would eventually be found to be physiological, and early introspective psychologists called their discipline Physiological Psychology. The theory of knowledge called Physicalism holds that when we introspect or have feelings we are looking at states or activities of our brains. But the major difficulties are practical: we cannot anticipate what a person will do by looking directly at his feelings *or* his nervous system, nor can we change his behavior by changing his mind *or* his brain. But in any case we seem to be no worse off for ignoring philosophical problems.

STRUCTURALISM

A more explicit strategy is to abandon the search for causes and simply describe what people do. Anthropologists can report customs and manners, political scientists can take the line of "behavioralism" and record political action, economists can amass statistics about what people buy and sell, rent and hire, save and spend, and make and consume, and psychologists can sample attitudes and opinions. All this may be done through direct observation, possibly with the help of recording systems, and with interviews, questionnaires, tests, and polls. The study of literature, art, and music is often confined to the forms of these products of human behavior, and linguists may confine themselves to phonetics, semantics, and syntax. A kind of prediction is possible on the principle that what people have often done they are likely to do again; they follow customs because it is customary to follow them, they exhibit voting or buying habits, and so on. The discovery of organizing principles in the structure of behavior—such as "universals" in cultures or languages, archetypal patterns in literature, or psychological types—may make it possible to predict instances of behavior that have not previously occurred.

The structure or organization of behavior can also be studied as a function of time or age, as in the development of a child's verbal behavior or his problem-solving strategies or in the sequence of stages through which a person passes on his way from infancy to maturity, or in the stages through which a culture evolves. History emphasizes changes occurring in time, and if patterns of development or growth can be discovered, they may also prove helpful in predicting future events.

Control is another matter. Avoiding mentalism (or "psychologism") by refusing to look at causes exacts its price. Structuralism and developmentalism do not tell us why customs are followed, why people vote as they do or display attitudes or traits of character, or why different languages have common features. Time or age cannot be manipulated; we can only wait for a person or a culture to pass through a developmental period.

In practice the systematic neglect of useful information has usually meant that the data supplied by the structuralist are acted upon by others—for example, by decision-makers who in some way manage to take the causes of behavior into account. In theory it has meant the survival of mentalistic concepts. When explanations are demanded, primitive cultural practices are attributed to "the mind of the savage," the acquisition of language to "innate rules of grammar," the development of problem-solving strategies to the "growth of mind," and so on. In short, structuralism tells us how people behave but throws very little light on why they behave as they do. It has no answer to the question with which we began.

METHODOLOGICAL BEHAVIORISM

The mentalistic problem can be avoided by going directly to the prior physical causes while bypassing intermediate feelings or states of mind. The quickest way to do this is to confine oneself to what an early behaviorist, Max Meyer, called the "psychology of the other one": consider only those facts which can be objectively observed in the behavior of one person in its relation to his prior environmental history. If all linkages are lawful, nothing is lost by neglecting a supposed nonphysical link. Thus, if we know that a child has not eaten for a long time, and if we know that he therefore feels hungry and that because he feels hungry he then eats, then we know that if he has not eaten for a long time, he will eat. And if by making other food inaccessible, we make him feel hungry, and if because he feels hungry he then eats a special food, then it must follow that by making other food inaccessible, we induce him to eat the special food.

Similarly, if certain ways of teaching a person lead him to notice very small differences in his "sensations," and if because he sees these differences he can classify colored objects correctly, then it should follow that we can use these ways of teaching him to classify objects correctly. Or, to take still another example, if circumstances in a white person's history generate feelings of aggression toward blacks, and if those feelings make him behave aggressively, then we may deal simply with the relation between the circumstances in his history and his aggressive behavior.

There is, of course, nothing new in trying to predict or control behavior by observing or manipulating prior public events. Structuralists and developmentalists have not entirely ignored the histories of their subjects, and historians and biographers have explored the influences of climate, culture, persons, and incidents. People have used practical techniques of predicting and controlling behavior with little thought to mental states. Nevertheless, for many centuries there was very little systematic inquiry into the role of the physical environment, although hundreds of highly technical volumes were written about human understanding and the life of the mind. A program of methodological behaviorism became plausible only when progress began to be made in the scientific observation of behavior, because only then was it possible to override the powerful effect of mentalism in diverting inquiry away from the role of the environment.

Mentalistic explanations allay curiosity and bring inquiry to a stop. It is so easy to observe feelings and states of mind at a time and in a place which make them seem like causes that we are not inclined to inquire further. Once the environment begins to be studied, however, its significance cannot be denied.

Methodological behaviorism might be thought of as a psychological version of logical positivism or operationism, but they are concerned with different issues. Logical positivism or operationism holds that since no two observers can agree on what happens in the world of the mind, then from the point of view of physical science mental events are "unobservables"; there can be no truth by agreement, and we must abandon the examination of mental events and turn instead to how they are studied. We cannot measure sensations and perceptions as such, but we can measure a person's capacity to discriminate among stimuli, and the *concept* of sensation or perception can then be reduced to the *operation* of discrimination.

The logical positivists had their version of "the other one." They argued that a robot which behaved precisely like a person, responding in the same way to stimuli, changing its behavior as a result of the same operations, would be indistinguishable from a real person, even though it would not have feelings, sensations, or ideas. If such a robot could be built, it would prove that none of the supposed manifestations of mental life demanded a mentalistic explanation.

With respect to its own goals, methodological behaviorism was successful. It disposed of many of the problems raised by mentalism and freed itself to work on its own projects without philosophical digressions. By directing attention to genetic and environmental antecedents, it offset an unwarranted concentration on an inner life. It freed us to study the behavior of lower species, where introspection (then regarded as exclusively human) was not feasible, and to explore similarities and differences between man and other species. Some concepts previously associated with private events were formulated in other ways.

But problems remained. Most methodological behaviorists granted the existence of mental events while ruling them out of consideration. Did they really mean to say that they did not matter, that the middle stage in that three-stage sequence of physical-mental-physical contributed nothing— in other words, that feelings and states of mind were merely epiphenomena? It was not the first time that anyone had said so. The view that a purely physical world could be self-sufficient had been suggested centuries before, in the doctrine of psychophysical parallelism, which held that there were two worlds—one of mind and one of matter—and that neither had any effect on the other. Freud's demonstration of the unconscious, in which an awareness of feelings or states of mind seemed unnecessary, pointed in the same direction.

But what about other evidence? Is the traditional *post hoc, ergo propter hoc* argument entirely wrong? Are the feelings we experience just before we behave wholly unrelated to our behavior? What about the power of mind over matter in psychosomatic medicine? What about psychophysics and the mathematical relation between the magnitudes of stimuli and sensations? What about the stream of consciousness? What about the intrapsychic processes of psychiatry, in which feelings produce or suppress other feelings and memories evoke or mask other memories? What about the cognitive processes said to explain perception, thinking, the construction of sentences, and artistic creation? Must all this be ignored because it cannot be studied objectively?

RADICAL BEHAVIORISM

The statement that behaviorists deny the existence of feelings, sensations, ideas, and other features of mental life needs a good deal of clarification. Methodological behaviorism and some versions of logical positivism ruled private events out of bounds because there could be no public agreement about their validity. Introspection could not be accepted as a scientific practice, and the psychology of people like Wilhelm Wundt and Edward B. Titchener was attacked accordingly. Radical behaviorism, however, takes a different line. It does not deny the possibility of self-observation or self-knowledge or its possible usefulness, but it questions the nature of what is felt or observed and hence known. It restores introspection but not what philosophers and introspective psychologists had believed they were "specting," and it raises the question of how much of one's body one can actually observe.

Mentalism kept attention away from the external antecedent events which might have explained behavior, by seeming to supply an alternative explanation. Methodological behaviorism did just the reverse: by dealing exclusively with external antecedent events it turned attention away from self-observation and self-knowledge. Radical behaviorism restores some kind of balance. It does not insist upon truth by agreement and can therefore consider events taking place in the private world within the skin. It does not call these events unobservable, and it does not dismiss them as subjective. It simply questions the nature of the

object observed and the reliability of the observations.
The position can be stated as follows: what is felt or introspectively observed is not some nonphysical world of consciousness, mind, or mental life but the observer's own body. This does not mean, as I shall show later, that introspection is a kind of physiological research, nor does it mean (and this is the heart of the argument) that what are felt or introspectively observed are the causes of behavior. An organism behaves as it does because of its current structure, but most of this is out of reach of introspection. At the moment we must content ourselves, as the methodological behaviorist insists, with a person's genetic and environmental histories. What are introspectively observed are certain collateral products of those histories.

The environment made its first great contribution during the evolution of the species, but it exerts a different kind of effect during the lifetime of the individual, and the combination of the two effects is the behavior we observe at any given time. Any available information about either contribution helps in the prediction and control of human behavior and in its interpretation in daily life. To the extent that either can be changed, behavior can be changed.

Our increasing knowledge of the control exerted by the environment makes it possible to examine the effect of the world within the skin and the nature of self-knowledge. It also makes it possible to interpret a wide range of mentalistic expressions. For example, we can look at those features of behavior which have led people to speak of an act of will, of a sense of purpose, of experience as distinct from reality, of innate or acquired ideas, of memories, meanings, and the personal knowledge of the scientist, and of hundreds of other mentalistic things or events. Some can be "translated into behavior," others discarded as unnecessary or meaningless.

In this way we repair the major damage wrought by mentalism. When what a person does is attributed to what is going on inside him, investigation is brought to an end. Why explain the explanation? For twenty-five hundred years people have been preoccupied with feelings and mental life, but only recently has any interest been shown in a more precise analysis of the role of the environment. Ignorance of that role led in the first place to mental fictions, and it has been perpetuated by the explanatory practices to which they gave rise.

A FEW WORDS OF CAUTION

As I noted in the Introduction, I am not speaking as *the* behaviorist. I believe I have written a consistent, coherent account, but it reflects my own environmental history. Bertrand Russell once pointed out that the experimental animals studied by American behaviorists behaved like Americans, running about in an almost random fashion, while those of Germans behaved like Germans, sitting and thinking. The remark may have been apt at the time, although it is meaningless today. Nevertheless, he was right in insisting that we are all culture-bound and that we approach the study of behavior with preconceptions. (And so, of course, do philosophers. Russell's account of how people think is very British, very Russellian. Mao Tse-tung's thoughts on the same subject are very Chinese. How could it be otherwise?)

I have not presupposed any technical knowledge on the part of the reader. A few facts and principles will, I hope, become familiar enough to be useful, since the discussion cannot proceed in a vacuum, but the book is not about a science of behavior but about its philosophy, and I have kept the scientific material to a bare minimum. Some terms appear many times, but it does not follow that the text is very repetitious. In later chapters, for example, the expression "contingencies of reinforcement" appears on almost every page, but contingencies are what the chapters are about. If they were about mushrooms, the word "mushroom" would be repeated as often.

Much of the argument goes beyond the established facts. I am concerned with interpretation rather than prediction and control. Every scientific field has a boundary beyond which discussion, though necessary, cannot be as precise as one would wish. One writer has recently said that "mere speculation which cannot be put to the test of experimental verification does not form part of science," but if that were true, a great deal of astronomy, for example, or atomic physics would not be science. Speculation is necessary, in fact, to devise methods which will bring a subject matter under better control.

I consider scores, if not hundreds, of examples of mentalistic usage. They are taken from current writing, but I have not cited the sources. I am not arguing with the authors but with the practices their terms or passages exemplify. I make the same use of examples as is made in a handbook of English usage. (I express my regrets if the authors would have preferred to be given credit, but I have applied the Golden Rule and have done unto others what I should have wished to have done if I had used such expressions.) Many of these expressions I "translate into behavior." I do so while acknowledging that *Traduttori traditori*—Translators are traitors—and that there are perhaps no exact behavioral equivalents, certainly none with the overtones and contexts of the originals. To spend much time on exact redefinitions of consciousness, will, wishes, sublimation, and so on would be as unwise as for physicists to do the same for ether, phlogiston, or *vis viva*.

Finally, a word about my own verbal behavior. The English language is heavy-laden with mentalism. Feelings and states of mind have enjoyed a commanding lead in the explanation of human behavior; and literature, preoccupied as it is with how and what people feel, offers continuing support. As a result, it is impossible to engage in casual discourse without raising the ghosts of mentalistic theories. The role of the environment was discovered very late, and no popular vocabulary has yet emerged.

For purposes of casual discourse I see no reason to avoid such an expression as "I have chosen to discuss . . ." (though I question the possibility of free choice), or "I have in mind . . ." (though I question the existence of a mind), or "I am aware of the fact . . ." (though I put a very special interpretation on awareness). The neophyte behaviorist is sometimes embarrassed when he finds himself using mentalistic terms, but the punishment of which his embarrassment is one effect is justified only when the terms are used in a technical discussion. When it is important to be clear about an issue, nothing but a technical vocabulary will suffice. It will often seem forced or roundabout. Old ways of speaking are abandoned with regret, and new ones are awkward and uncomfortable, but the change must be made.

This is not the first time a science has suffered from such a transition. There were periods when it was difficult for the astronomer not to sound like an astrologer (or to be an astrologer at heart) and when the chemist had by no means freed himself from alchemy. We are in a similar stage in a science of behavior, and the sooner the transition is completed the better. The practical consequences are easily demonstrated: education, politics, psychotherapy, penology, and many other fields of human affairs are suffering from the eclectic use of a lay vocabulary. The theoretical consequences are harder to demonstrate but, as I hope to show in what follows, equally important.

2

The World Within the Skin

A small part of the universe is contained within the skin of each of us. There is no reason why it should have any special physical status because it lies within this boundary, and eventually we should have a complete account of it from anatomy and physiology. No very good account is now available, however, and it therefore seems all the more important that we should be in touch with it in other ways. We feel it and in some sense observe it, and it would seem foolish to neglect this source of information just because no more than one person can make contact with one inner world. Nevertheless, our behavior in making that contact needs to be examined.

We respond to our own body with three nervous systems, two of which are particularly concerned with internal features. The so-called interoceptive system carries stimulation from organs like the bladder and alimentary tract, from glands and their ducts, and from blood vessels. It is primarily important for the internal economy of the organism.

The so-called proprioceptive system carries stimulation from the muscles, joints, and tendons of the skeletal frame and from other organs involved in the maintenance of posture and the execution of movement. We use the verb "feel" in describing our contact with these two kinds of stimulation. A third nervous system, the exteroceptive, is primarily concerned with seeing, hearing, tasting, smelling, and feeling things in the world around us, but it also plays an important part in observing our own body.

OBSERVING AND DESCRIBING THE WORLD WITHIN THE SKIN

All three nervous systems presumably evolved to their present condition because they served important biological functions, but they came to serve another function with the appearance of verbal behavior. People eventually asked questions of each other, the answers to which called for a different kind of responding to the body. Questions such as "Are you hungry?", "Does your head ache?", "What are you doing?", "What do you plan to do tomorrow?", "What did you do yesterday?", and "Why are you doing that?" evoke answers which are useful in predicting and preparing for what a person will do, and they seem to give information about a world beyond the reach of other people.

We might expect that because a person is in such intimate contact with his own body he should be able to describe its conditions and processes particularly well, but the very privacy which seems to confer a special privilege on the individual makes it difficult for the community to teach him to make distinctions. The community can teach a child to name colors in various ways. For example, it can show him colored objects, ask him to respond with color words, and commend or correct him when his responses correspond or fail to correspond with the colors of the objects. If the child has normal color vision, we expect him to learn to identify colors accurately. The community cannot, however, follow the same practice in teaching him to describe the states of his own body because it lacks the information it needs to commend or correct him

REPORTING THINGS FELT

Fortunately, it does not follow that no one can learn to describe some of the states of his own body, because the verbal community can to some extent solve the problem of privacy. For example, it can teach responses descriptive of internal conditions by using associated public conditions. Something of the sort happens when a blind person is taught to name the objects he feels by a teacher who merely sees the objects. The teacher can commend or correct him because the visual and tactual stimuli are almost perfectly correlated. The verbal community follows a rather similar practice when it teaches a child such an expression as "That hurts." When the child has received a sharp blow or cut, the public blow or cut is fairly reliably associated with the private stimuli generated by it. The verbal community uses the public information, but the child may eventually say "That hurts" while responding only to the private event. He has learned to describe a private stimulus with an accuracy which depends only upon how well the public and private events agree.

The practice explains why terms which describe pains almost always describe their public causes. "Pain" itself comes from the Greek and Latin for punishment. A sharp pain is the pain produced by a sharp object; a dull pain by a dull object. Pains can be wrenching or piercing; a headache may pound; and "excruciating" is related to crucifixion. We often ask about feelings by asking, "What does it feel *like?*" and the answer usually refers to a public condition which often produces a similar private effect. Thus, a person who has had a stroke of luck may say, "I feel as if I'd won a million dollars." A standard literary practice is to describe feelings by describing conditions which are likely to arouse similar feelings. Keats reported what it felt like when he first looked into Chapman's translation of Homer, in the following way:

> Then felt I like some watcher of the skies
> When a new planet swims into his ken;
> Or like stout Cortez, when with eagle eyes
> He star'd at the Pacific—

The verbal community may also circumvent the restrictions imposed by privacy by using collateral responses to the stimuli which a person is to learn to identify or describe. For example, it may observe not only that a child receives a painful blow, but that he cries. The private stimuli which come to control the response "That hurts" are then less likely to be described with terms first descriptive of public stimuli. Similarly, although the community may teach a child to say, "I am hungry," because it knows that the child has not eaten for a long time, it is much more likely to take advantage of collateral behavior: it observes that the child responds quickly or eats ravenously when given food. It then tells him that he is hungry, and the child may acquire the expression "I am hungry" with respect to collateral private stimuli to which the verbal community had no access.

Terms referring to emotional or motivational states often show some connection with the external circumstances responsible for them. For example, we feel *sad* in the original sense of *sated*, or *excited* in the sense of *stirred up*, but these expressions may be little more than metaphors. We are not tense in the literal sense of being stretched, or depressed in the literal sense of weighed down. We may have acquired these words under circumstances which have no connection with behavior or feelings. Almost all terms descriptive of emotions which do not carry a direct reference to inciting conditions were originally metaphors.

Although the verbal community solves the problem of privacy in this way and succeeds in teaching a person to describe many states of his body, the descriptions are never completely accurate. The physician allows for considerable latitude when his patient describes his aches and pains. The difficulty is not that the patient is not being stimulated in a perfectly clear way, it is simply that he has never been exposed to instructional conditions under which he has learned to describe the stimuli adequately. Moreover—and this is a point of the greatest importance, to which I shall return later—the original biological functions responsible for the evolution of the nervous system have not produced the system the verbal community needs. As a result, we are particularly likely to distrust reports of private stimulation, especially when a description has other consequences—as, for example, in malingering.

REPORTING BEHAVIOR

Current Behavior.   The question "What are you doing?" asks for information which may be quite public but which is at the moment out of reach of the questioner, who may be speaking over the telephone, for example, or in the dark, or around a corner. The vocabulary in which the answer is given can be acquired when the behavior is visible to all parties, and the verbal community therefore suffers no limitation. Descriptions may be confined to topography ("I am waving my hand") or may include effects on the environment ("I am drinking a glass of water" or "I am sewing a button on my shirt"). Proprioceptive stimuli are dominant when a person describes his own behavior in the dark, but they are closely related to the public stimuli used in instruction by the verbal community. Questions of this sort are asked because the answers are important to the community, but, as we shall see later, they also become important to the speaker himself and in ways which are likely to maintain their accuracy.

Probable Behavior.   "What are you inclined to do?" is a metaphorical question, to which a metaphorical answer might be "I lean toward going." To *tend* to do something is also a metaphor, suggesting being pulled or stretched. Answers presumably depend upon stimulation generated by conditions associated with a marked probability of action. When something funny happens on a solemn occasion, we may report, "I felt like laughing" or, "I wanted to laugh" or, "I could scarcely keep from laughing." The stimulation thus described presumably accompanied earlier instances when laughter occurred and a suitable vocabulary was acquired.

Perceptual Behavior.   A person may be asked, "Do you see that?" or, less idiomatically, "Are you seeing that?" and the answer may be checked by asking for the name or a description of what is seen.

Past Behavior.   Answers to such questions as "What did you do yesterday?" or "Whom did you see?" can use a vocabulary acquired in connection with current behavior. A person simply speaks from a special vantage point: he was necessarily there. Such questions are scarcely different from, say, "What happened yesterday?" (Whether it is easier to describe yesterday's behavior if one also described it yesterday is a matter of some importance. It has been suggested, for example, that we do not remember what happened in infancy because we were not able to describe it at that time ["infant" once meant "incapable of speech"], but we do not constantly describe the behavior we are engaging in although we can usually describe it later. Nevertheless, the quick forgetting of dreams and of passing thoughts which have not been clearly "noted" suggests that a current running account is the best way to make sure that behavior can be described at a later date.)

Covert Behavior.   A much more difficult question is "What are you thinking?" where "thinking" refers to behavior executed on such a small scale that it is not visible to others. (Other uses of the word "think" are discussed in Chapter 7.) In describing covert behavior we may be describing public behavior in miniature, but it is more likely that we are describing private conditions associated with public behavior but not necessarily generated by it. Verbal behavior can easily become covert because it does not require environmental support. "I said to myself . . ." is used synonymously with "I thought . . . ," but we do not say, "I swam to myself."

Covert perceptual behavior is especially puzzling. Imagining or fantasying, as ways of "seeing" something in the absence of the thing seen, are presumably a matter of doing what one does when what is seen is present. I shall return to this point in Chapter 5.

The verbal community may resort to instrumental amplification, as of the activity of muscles, and thus in a sense make covert behavior public, and encourage a return to the overt level as by asking a person to "think out loud," but it cannot maintain the accuracy of covert behavior. There is no problem, however, in the provenance of the vocabulary. The words used to describe covert behavior are the words acquired when behaving publicly.

Future Behavior.   Another difficult question is "What are you going to do?" The answer is, of course, not a description of the future behavior itself. It may be a report of strong covert behavior likely to be emitted publicly when the occasion arises ("When I see him, I shall remind him that he owes me ten dollars"). It may be a prediction of behavior based on current conditions with which the behavior is often associated ("When things are like this, I generally give up" or "I'm hungry and I am going to get something to eat"). It may be a report of a strong probability of behaving in a given way.

Statements about future behavior often involve the word "feel." Perhaps "I feel like playing cards" may be translated as "I feel as I often feel when I have started to play cards." "What do you *want* to do?" may refer to the future in the sense of asking about the probability of behavior.

An attitude ("Do you really want to do what you are doing?" or "Do you really want to go to the beach for your vacation?") may be part of the metaphor of inclination or tendency.

In general the verbal community can check the accuracy of statements regarding inclinations and tendencies, at least in a statistical way, by looking at what happens, and the accuracy of the control maintained by private stimuli is thus to some extent assured. We shall see that self-descriptive behavior also serves the individual himself and that when it does so, it tends to remain accurate.

Multiple Translations.   Conditions relevant to behavior are reported according to the circumstances in which they have been acquired, and this means that an expression may be translated in several ways. Consider the report "I am, was, or will be hungry." "I am hungry" may be equivalent to "I have hunger pangs," and if the verbal community had some means of observing the contractions of the stomach associated with pangs, it could pin the response to these stimuli alone. It may also be equivalent to "I am eating actively." A person who observes that he is eating voraciously may say, "I really am hungry," or, in retrospect, "I was hungrier than I thought," dismissing other evidence as unreliable. "I am hungry" may also be equivalent to "It has been a long time since I have had anything to eat," although the expression is most likely to be used in describing future behavior: "If I miss my dinner, I shall be hungry." "I am hungry" may also be equivalent to "I feel like eating" in the sense of "I have felt this way before when I have started to eat." It may be equivalent to "I am covertly engaging in behavior similar to that involved in getting and consuming food" or "I am fantasying eating" or "I am thinking of things I like to eat" or "I am 'eating to myself.' " To say, "I am hungry," may be to report several or all of these conditions.

IDENTIFYING THE CAUSES OF ONE'S BEHAVIOR

"What are you doing?" is frequently a request for further information. The question might be asked of someone who is rummaging a box of small objects, and a characteristic response might be "I am looking for my old pocketknife." The word "rummaging" describes a particular kind of behavior; in addition to a particular topography, it implies a reason. A person who is rummaging is looking for something, and the rummaging will cease when it is found. A different question, "What are you looking for?" narrows the field, and "My old pocketknife" identifies the object sought, the finding of which will bring the behavior to an end. A further question, "Why are you looking for your knife?" might call out the answer "Because I want it," which usually means more than "Because it is wanting."

A more direct question about causes is "Why are you doing that?" and the answer is usually a description of feelings: "Because I feel like doing it." Such an answer is often acceptable, but if the verbal community insists upon something else, it may ask, "Why do you feel like doing it?" and the answer will then be either a reference to other feelings or (at long last) to external circumstances. Thus, in reply to "Why are you moving your chair?", a person may say, "The light was bad" or "To get a better light on my book."

Questions of this kind are not always correctly answered, since we often do not know why we behave as we do. In spite of the apparent intimacy of the world within the skin, and in spite of the advantage a person enjoys as an observer of his personal history, another person may know more about why he behaves. The psychotherapist who attempts to give his patient insight is presumably emphasizing causal relationships of which his patient is not yet aware.

When we do not know why we behave, we are likely to invent causes: "I did it, so I must have thought it would help." It is possible that many myths are little more than invented causes of the superstitious behavior, seemingly uncaused, to be discussed in Chapter 8.

Explanations of behavior vary with the kinds of answers accepted by the verbal community. If a simple "I feel like it" suffices, nothing else will appear. Freud was influential in changing the kinds of answers often given to "Why are you doing that?" He emphasized feelings but allowed for references to personal history. The experimental analysis of behavior goes directly to the antecedent causes in the environment.

SELF-KNOWLEDGE

I have been emphasizing a difference between feelings and reporting what one feels. We may take feeling to be simply responding to stimuli, but reporting is the product of the special verbal contingencies arranged by a community. There is a similar difference between behaving and reporting that one is behaving or reporting the causes of one's behavior. In arranging conditions under which a person describes the public or private world in which he lives, a community generates that very special form of behavior called knowing. Responding to an empty stomach by getting and ingesting food is one thing; knowing that one is hungry is another. Walking over rough terrain is one thing; knowing that one is doing so is another.

Self-knowledge is of social origin. It is only when a person's private world becomes important to others that it is made important to him. It then enters into the control of the behavior called knowing. But self-knowledge has a special value to the individual himself. A person who has been "made aware of himself" by the questions he has been asked is in a better position to predict and control his own behavior.

A behavioristic analysis does not question the practical usefulness of reports of the inner world that is felt and introspectively observed. They are clues (1) to past behavior and the conditions affecting it, (2) to current behavior and the conditions affecting it, and (3) to conditions related to future behavior. Nevertheless, the private world within the skin is not clearly observed or known. I have mentioned two reasons, to which I shall have many occasions to return: in teaching self-knowledge (1) the verbal community must make do with rather primitive nervous systems, and (2) it cannot fully solve the problem of privacy. There is an old principle that nothing is different until it makes a difference, and with respect to events in the world within the skin the verbal community has not been able to make things different enough. As a result, there is room for speculation, which over the centuries has shown the most extraordinary diversity.

Plato is said to have discovered the mind, but it would be more accurate to say that he invented one version of it. Long before his time, the Greeks had constructed an elaborate explanatory system, a strange mixture of physiology and metaphysics. A pure mentalism was not long in making its appearance, and it has dominated Western thinking for more than two thousand years. Almost all versions contend that the mind is a nonphysical space in which events obey nonphysical laws. The "consciousness" of which a person is said to be aware has become such a staple of Western thinking that "everyone knows what it means to be conscious," and the behaviorist who raises a question is called disingenuous, as if he were refusing to admit the evidence of his senses.

Even those who insist upon the reality of mental life will usually agree that little or no progress has been made since Plato's day. Mentalistic theories are subject to changes in fashion and, as in the history of clothing or architecture, one has only to wait long enough to find an earlier view back in style. We have had Aristotelian revivals and are now said to be returning to Plato. Modern psychology can claim to be far beyond Plato in controlling the environments of which people are said to be conscious, but it has not greatly improved their access to consciousness itself, because it has not been able to improve the verbal contingencies under which feelings and states of mind are described and known. One has only to look at any half-dozen current mentalistic theories to see how much variety is still possible.

Behaviorism, on the other hand, has moved forward. Profiting from recent advances in the experimental analysis of behavior, it has looked more closely at the conditions under which people respond to the world within their skin, and it can now analyze, one by one, the key terms in the mentalistic armamentarium. What follows is offered as an example.

3

Innate Behavior

The human species, like all other species, is the product of natural selection. Each of its members is an extremely complex organism, a living system, the subject of anatomy and physiology. Fields such as respiration, digestion, circulation, and immunization have been set apart for special study, and among them is the field we call behavior.

It usually involves the environment. The newborn infant is so constructed that it takes in air and food and puts out wastes. Breathing, suckling, urination, and defecation are things the newborn infant *does,* but so, of course, are all its other physiological activities.

When we know enough about the anatomy and physiology of the newborn, we shall be able to say *why* it breathes, suckles, urinates, and defecates, but at the moment we must be content with describing the behavior itself and investigating the conditions under which it occurs—such as external or internal stimulation, age, or level of deprivation.

33

REFLEXES AND RELEASED BEHAVIORS

One kind of relation between behavior and stimulation is called a reflex. As soon as the word was coined, it was taken to refer to the underlying anatomy and physiology, but these are still only roughly known. At the moment a reflex has only a descriptive force; it is not an explanation. To say that a baby breathes or suckles because it possesses appropriate reflexes is simply to say that it breathes or suckles, presumably because it has evolved in such a way that it does so. Breathing and suckling involve responses to the environment, but in no other way are they to be distinguished from the rest of respiration and digestion.

When reflexes first began to be studied in isolated parts of the organism, the results were felt to challenge the role of inner determiners of conduct. Some reflexes, for example, seemed to displace the *Rüchenmarkseele*—the soul, or mind, of the spinal cord—the defense of which was an early attack on an environmental analysis.

Behavior usually involves the environment in a more complex way. Well-known examples are found in lower species. Courting, mating, building nests, and caring for young are things organisms *do,* and again presumably because of the way they have evolved. Behavior of this sort is usually called instinctive rather than reflexive, and the ethologist speaks of the environment as "releasing" behavior, a less compelling action than eliciting a reflex response. Released, or instinctive, behavior is also more flexible than reflexive in adapting to adventitious features of the environment. But to say that a bird builds a nest because it possesses a nest-building instinct, or because certain conditions release nest building, is merely to describe the fact, not to explain it. Instinctive behavior presents a more complex assignment for the physiologist than reflex, and at the moment we have few relevant facts and can only speculate about the kinds of systems which may be involved.

When we say that a good prose stylist has an "instinct" which permits him to judge without reflection that a sentence is well written, we mean nothing more than that he possesses certain deeply ingrained behavior of uncertain provenance. We often mean little more in speaking of instincts in general, and there is perhaps no harm in using the word in this way, but much more is often read into the term. A reflex has been described by saying that "stimuli initiate a state of tension that seeks discharge, bringing about relaxation." "Every instance of instinctive behavior," said William McDougall, "involves the knowing of some thing or object, a feeling in regard to it, and a striving towards or away from that object." Feelings are ascribed to the behaving organism when it is said that the moth likes the light it flies toward or bees the appearance and odor of the flowers they frequent. The difficulties raised by the key terms in sentences of that sort—tension, discharge, relaxation, knowing, feeling, striving, and liking—will be considered in later chapters.

Instincts as Driving Forces.   A more serious mistake is made in converting an instinct into a force. We are not likely to speak of a force in explaining the fact than an organism digests its food or develops immunity to a disease, but the notion often appears in discussing the organism's relation to its environment. Herbert Spencer's "life force," Schopenhauer's "blind will to exist," and Bergson's *"élan vital"* were early examples of the conversion of biological processes into more energetic or substantial forms. The *élan vital,* for example, was said to be "a tireless power continually driving onward and upward." The Freudian instincts were also treated as driving forces; behavior which led to danger, ill health, or death was said to show a death instinct, while behavior said to be "in the service of life" showed a life instinct, although the observed fact was simply that behavior might have sustaining or destructive consequences.

Two examples which have recently attracted a good deal of attention may be noted: (1) When injured or threatened, an organism is likely to attack—for example, by striking or biting—and, as I shall argue in a moment, some behavior of this sort may be as much a part of the genetic endowment as respiration or digestion, but we have no reason to say that an organism attacks *because* it possesses an aggressive instinct. The attack is the only evidence we have of the tendency to attack. (2) Some species defend the territories in which they live, and some of the behavior seems to be due to a genetic endowment, but to say that an organism defends its territory *because* of a territorial imperative or any other kind of instinct is simply to say that it is the kind of organism which defends it territory. (The expression "genetic endowment" is itself dangerous. Like reflexes and instincts, it tends to acquire properties not warranted by the evidence and to begin to serve as a cause rather than as representing the current effects of natural selection, from which attention is then deflected.)

Darwin's theory of natural selection came very late in the history of thought. Was it delayed because it opposed revealed truth, because it was an entirely new subject in the history of science, because it was characteristic only of living things, or because it dealt with purpose and final causes without postulating an act of creation? I think not. Darwin simply discovered the role of selection, a kind of causality very different from the push-pull mechanisms of science up to that time. The origin of a fantastic variety of living things could be explained by the contribution which novel features, possibly of random provenance, made to survival. There was little or nothing in physical or biological science that foreshadowed selection as a causal principle.

Although we still do not know much about the anatomy and physiology underlying behavior, we can speculate about the process of selection which made them part of a genetic endowment. Survival may be said to be *contingent upon* certain kinds of behavior. For example, if members of a species did not mate, care for their young, or defend themselves against predators, the species would not survive. It is not easy to study these "contingencies of survival" experimentally because selection is a slow process, but some effects may be shown by studying species which quickly mature to breeding age and by carefully arranging conditions of selection.

Contingencies of survival are often described with terms which suggest a different kind of causal action. "Selection pressure" is an example. Selection is a special kind of causality which is not properly represented as a force or pressure. To say that there is "no obvious selection pressure on mammals that explains the high level of intelligence reached by primates" is simply to say that it is hard to imagine conditions under which slightly more intelligent members of a species would be more likely to survive. (What is wrong, by the way, is the suggestion that "pressure" is exerted primarily by other species. Survival may depend almost wholly on "competing with" the physical environment, when intelligent behavior is clearly favored.)

Contingencies of survival are more easily imagined if the behavior makes it more probable that individuals will survive and breed and if the contingencies prevail over long periods of time. Conditions within the body have usually satisfied both these requirements, and some features of the external environment, such as the cycles of day and night, or the seasons, or temperature, or the gravitational field, are long-lasting. And so are other members of the same species, a fact which explains the prominence given by ethologists to courtship, sex, parental care, social behavior, play, imitation, and aggression. But plausible conditions of selection are hard to find in support of such an assertion as that "principles of grammar are present in the mind at birth," since grammatical behavior can hardly have been sufficiently important to survival, for a long enough time, to explain its selection. As I shall note again later, verbal behavior could arise only when the necessary ingredients had already evolved for other reasons.

PREPARATION FOR NEW ENVIRONMENTS
I: RESPONDENT CONDITIONING

Contingencies of survival cannot produce useful behavior if the environment changes substantially from generation to generation, but certain mechanisms have evolved by virtue of which the individual acquires behavior appropriate to a novel environment during his lifetime. The conditioned reflex is a relatively simple example. Certain cardiac reflexes support strong exertion, as in running away from or struggling with a predator; and there is presumably an advantage if the heart responds before running or struggling begins; but predators vary in appearance, and it is only through respondent conditioning that a particular appearance can elicit appropriate cardiac behavior in advance of running or struggling.

A conditioned reflex, as a thing a person possesses, has no more explanatory force than an unconditioned or innate reflex. The heart of the runner does not begin to beat strongly and rapidly just before a race *because* of the conditioned cardiac reflex; the reflex is simply a way of identifying the fact that it begins to beat rapidly. The runner has been changed when situations at the start of a race have been followed by strong exertion, and as a changed organism he behaves in a different way. It is merely convenient to identify the change as the "acquisition of a conditioned reflex."

Just as we point to contingencies of survival to explain an unconditioned reflex, so we can point to "contingencies of reinforcement" to explain a conditioned reflex. Reflex phenomena, conditioned and unconditioned, have, of course, been known for centuries, but it is only recently that contingencies of survival and contingencies of reinforcement have been investigated.

Inner Supplements. The conditioned reflex is a simple principle of limited scope describing certain simple facts, but many internal states and activities, comparable with the driving force of instincts, have been invented to explain it. The runner's heart is said to beat fast before the start of the race because he "associates" the situation with the exertion which follows. But it is the environment, not the runner, that "associates" the two features, in the etymological sense of joining or uniting them. Nor does the runner "form a connection" between the two things; the connection is made in the external world. Conditioned responses are also said to occur in "anticipation" of, or in "expectation" of, customary consequences, and the conditioned stimulus is said to function as a "sign," "signal," or "symbol." I shall return to these expressions later.

PREPARATION FOR NEW ENVIRONMENTS
II: OPERANT CONDITIONING

A very different process, through which a person comes to deal effectively with a new environment, is operant conditioning. Many things in the environment, such as food and water, sexual contact, and escape from harm, are crucial for the survival of the individual and the species, and any behavior which produces them therefore has survival value. Through the process of operant conditioning, behavior having this kind of consequence becomes more likely to occur. The behavior is said to be *strengthened* by its consequences, and for that reason the consequences themselves are called "reinforcers." Thus, when a hungry organism exhibits behavior that *produces* food, the behavior is reinforced by that consequence and is therefore more likely to recur. Behavior that *reduces* a potentially damaging condition, such as an extreme of temperature, is reinforced by that consequence and therefore tends to recur on similar occasions. The process and its effects have given rise to a large number of mentalistic concepts, many of which will be examined in the following chapters.

The standard distinction between operant and reflex behavior is that one is voluntary and the other involuntary. Operant behavior is felt to be under the control of the behaving person and has traditionally been attributed to an act of will. Reflex behavior, on the other hand, is not under comparable control and has even been attributed to invading wills, such as those of possessing spirits. Sneezing, hiccuping, and other reflex acts were once attributed to the Devil, from whom we still protect a friend who has sneezed by saying, "God bless you!" (Montaigne said he crossed himself even when he yawned.) When no invader is assumed, the behavior is simply called automatic.

INTERMINGLING OF CONTINGENCIES OF SURVIVAL AND REINFORCEMENT

There are certain remarkable similarities between contingencies of survival and contingencies of reinforcement. Both exemplify, as I have noted, a kind of causality which was discovered very late in the history of human thought. Both account for purpose by moving it after the fact, and both are relevant to the question of a creative design. When we have reviewed the contingencies which generate new forms of behavior in the individual, we shall be in a better position to evaluate those which generate innate behavior in the species. Meanwhile we may note the importance of insisting upon the distinction.

Imprinting.   Operant conditioning and natural selection are combined in the so-called imprinting of a newly hatched duckling. In its natural environment, the young duckling moves toward its mother and follows her as she moves about. The behavior has obvious survival value. When no duck is present, the duckling behaves in much the same way with respect to other objects. (In *Utopia*, Thomas More reported, the chicks hatched in an incubator followed those who fed and cared for them.) Recently it has been shown that a young duckling will come to approach and follow any moving object, particularly if it is about the same size as a duck—for example, a shoe box. Evidently survival is sufficiently well served even if the behavior is not under the control of the specific visual features of a duck. Merely approaching and following is enough.

Even so, that is not a correct statement of what happens. What the duckling inherits is the capacity to be reinforced by maintaining or reducing the distance between itself and a moving object. In the natural environment, and in the laboratory in which imprinting is studied, approaching and following have these consequences, but the contingencies can be changed. A mechanical system can be constructed in which movement *toward* an object causes the object to move rapidly away, while movement *away from* the object causes it to come closer. Under these conditions, the duckling will move away from the object rather than approach or follow it. A duckling will learn to peck a spot on the wall if pecking brings the object closer. Only by knowing what and how the duckling learns during its lifetime can we be sure of what it is equipped to do at birth.

Imitation and the Instinct of the Herd.   Natural selection and operant conditioning are often confused when they produce behaviors having similar topographies. The survival value of behaving as others behave seems obvious. If one member of a group responds to an approaching predator by flying, running, or swimming away, and the rest of the group then does the same, all may reach safety although only one has made direct contact with the predator. The conditions are suitable for natural selection because other members are an enduring part of the environment of a species. Nevertheless, very similar behavior is produced by contingencies of reinforcement. In general when a person is behaving in a given way, he is doing so because of prevailing contingencies, and similar behavior on the part of another person in the same situation is likely to be subject to the same contingencies. If one observes people running down a street, one may respond indirectly to the same contingencies by running with them, thereby possibly escaping danger or discovering something interesting. To speak of an instinct of "imitation" or an "instinct of the herd" is ambiguous; it may refer to contingencies of survival or contingencies of reinforcement.

Territoriality and Aggression. These terms do not refer to specific forms of behavior. An organism may defend its territory or attack others in many different ways. Modern warfare is often said to exemplify territoriality and aggression, but it would be hard to find any act of a soldier that could have been selected by contingencies of survival. At best, warlike behavior is acquired because of an inherent capacity to be reinforced by gains in territory or damage inflicted upon others.

Aggressive behavior may be innate and released by specific circumstances in which survival value is plausible. An infant or child may bite, scratch, or strike if physically restrained when it could not have learned to do so. Or the behavior may be shaped and maintained because people are susceptible to reinforcement by signs of damage to others. The capacity to be reinforced when an opponent cries out or runs away would have survival value because a person so endowed would quickly learn to defend himself. Or, third, the behavior may be reinforced by consequences not explicitly related to aggression. Food and sexual contact, reinforcing for other reasons, may reinforce an attack on a competitor if food or a sexual partner is thus obtained.

The intermingling of contingencies of survival and reinforcement causes trouble, and it is not surprising that nativists and environmentalists often disagree and sometimes rather aggressively defend their respective territories.

Species-Specific "Universals."   The term "instinct" is sometimes avoided by referring instead to species-specific behavior on the theory that something characteristic of all members of a species is probably part of its genetic endowment. But contingencies of reinforcement are species-specific too. We have seen an example in the behavior of the duckling that follows its mother because of the "universal" fact that moving in the direction of an object normally brings it closer. Universal features of language do not imply a universal innate endowment, because the contingencies of reinforcement arranged by verbal communities have universal features. Psychoanalysts have made a great deal of the universality of the Oedipus complex, but the contingencies of personal reinforcement in the family in a given culture may be equally universal.

The Importance of Maintaining the Distinction.   It is no doubt true that early behaviorists were unduly enthusiastic about the learning processes they were discovering and neglected the role of behavioral genetics, but reactions to the behaviorist position have also been marked by exaggeration. There is no longer any need for controversy, even though we are still a long way from understanding all the interactions between contingencies of survival and contingencies of reinforcement.

In an important sense all behavior is inherited, since the organism that behaves is the product of natural selection. Operant conditioning is as much a part of the genetic endowment as digestion or gestation. The question is not whether the human species has a genetic endowment but how it is to be analyzed. It begins and remains a biological system, and the behavioristic position is that it is nothing more than that.

Quite apart from the details of the resulting behavior, there are good reasons for distinguishing between the two kinds of contingencies. They differ greatly in their bearing on the question with which we began: Why do people behave as they do? Contingencies of reinforcement have the edge with respect to prediction and control. The conditions under which a person acquires behavior are relatively accessible and can often be manipulated; the conditions under which a species acquires behavior are very nearly out of reach. One unfortunate consequence is that genetic sources sometimes become a kind of dumping ground: any aspect of behavior which at the moment escapes analysis in terms of contingencies of reinforcement is likely to be assigned to genetic endowment, and we are likely to accept the explanation because we are so accustomed to going no further than a state of the organism.

"THE EVOLUTION OF MIND"

The concept of mind had been thoroughly elaborated before the advent of evolutionary theory, and some accommodation was needed. When and how did mind evolve? What kind of mutation could have given rise to the first mental state or process which, in contributing to the survival of the person in whom it occurred, became part of the human genetic endowment? The question is not unlike that raised by the conversion of reality into experience or of thought into action. What sort of physical gene could carry the potential of mind, and how could mind satisfy physical contingencies of survival? If mind is nothing more than a manifestation of physiology, such questions can be answered, or at least postponed without anxiety until physiology can answer them, but not all who subscribe to mentalism accept that position. Mind has been said by some—Teilhard de Chardin, for example—to be the end and purpose of evolution, if not something beyond it. The distinguished scientist Vannevar Bush has put it this way:

> We seem, thus, to have arrived at a concept of how the physical universe about us—all the life that inhabits the speck we occupy in this universe—has evolved over the eons of time by simple material processes, the sort of processes we examine experimentally, which we describe by equations, and call the "laws of nature." Except for one thing! Man is conscious of his existence. Man also possesses, so most of us believe, what he calls his free will. Did consciousness and free will too arise merely out of "natural" processes? The question is central to the contention between those who see nothing beyond a new materialism and those who see—Something.

The behaviorist has a simpler answer. What has evolved is an organism, part of the behavior of which has been tentatively explained by the invention of the concept of mind. No special evolutionary process is needed when the facts are considered in their own right.

Operant Behavior

The process of operant conditioning described in the preceding chapter is simple enough. When a bit of behavior has the kind of consequence called reinforcing, it is more likely to occur again. A positive reinforcer strengthens any behavior that produces it: a glass of water is positively reinforcing when we are thirsty, and if we then draw and drink a glass of water, we are more likely to do so again on similar occasions. A negative reinforcer strengthens any behavior that reduces or terminates it: when we take off a shoe that is pinching, the reduction in pressure is negatively reinforcing, and we are more likely to do so again when a shoe pinches.

The process supplements natural selection. Important consequences of behavior which could not play a role in evolution because they were not sufficiently stable features of the environment are made effective through operant conditioning during the lifetime of the individual, whose power in dealing with his world is thus vastly increased.

THE FEELINGS OF REINFORCERS

The fact that operant conditioning, like all physiological processes, is a product of natural selection throws light on the question of what kinds of consequences are reinforcing and why. It is commonly said that a thing is reinforcing because it feels, looks, sounds, smells, or tastes good, but from the point of view of evolutionary theory a susceptibility to reinforcement is due to its survival value and not to any associated feelings.

The point may be made for the reinforcers which play a part in the conditioning of reflexes. Salivation is elicited by certain chemical stimuli on the tongue (as other secretions are elicited by other stimuli in later stages of digestion) because the effect has contributed to the survival of the species. A person may report that a substance tastes good, but it does not elicit salivation because it tastes good. Similarly, we pull our hand away from a hot object, but not because the object *feels* painful. The behavior occurs because appropriate mechanisms have been selected in the course of evolution. The feelings are merely collateral products of the conditions responsible for the behavior.

The same may be said of operant reinforcers. Salt and sugar are critical requirements, and individuals who were especially likely to be reinforced by them have more effectively learned and remembered where and how to get them and have therefore been more likely to survive and transmit this susceptibility to the species. It has often been pointed out that competition for a mate tends to select the more skillful and powerful members of a species, but it also selects those more susceptible to sexual reinforcement. As a result, the human species, like other species, is powerfully reinforced by sugar, salt, and sexual contact. This is very different from saying that these things reinforce *because* they taste or feel good.

Feelings have dominated the discussion of rewards and

punishments for centuries. One reason is that the conditions we report when we say that a taste, odor, sound, picture, or piece of music is delicious, pleasant, or beautiful are part of the immediate situation, whereas the effect they may have in changing our behavior is much less salient—and much less likely to be "seen," because the verbal environment cannot establish good contingencies. According to the philosophy of hedonism, people act to achieve pleasure and escape from or avoid pain, and the effects referred to in Edward L. Thorndike's famous Law of Effect were feelings: "satisfying" or "annoying." The verb "to like" is a synonym of "to be pleased with"; we say "If you like" and "If you please" more or less interchangeably.

Some of these terms refer to other effects of reinforcers—satisfying, for example, is related to satiation—but most refer to the bodily states generated by reinforcers. It is sometimes possible to discover what reinforces a person simply by asking him what he likes or how he feels about things. What we learn is similar to what we learn by testing the effect of a reinforcer: he is talking about what has reinforced him in the past or what he sees himself "going for." But this does not mean that his feelings are causally effective; his answer reports a collateral effect.

The expressions "I like Brahms," "I love Brahms," "I enjoy Brahms," and "Brahms pleases me" may easily be taken to refer to feelings, but they can be regarded as statements that the music of Brahms is reinforcing. A person of whom the expressions are true will listen to the radio when it plays Brahms rather than turn it off, buy and play records of Brahms, and go to concerts where Brahms is played. The expressions have antonyms ("I dislike Brahms," "I hate Brahms," "I detest Brahms," and "Brahms bores me"), and a person for whom Brahms is thus aversive will act to avoid or escape from hearing him. These expressions do not refer to instances of reinforcement but rather to a general susceptibility or the lack of it.

The allusion to what is felt needs to be carefully examined. Feelings are especially plausible when the experience is directed toward a living person. The statement "I love my wife" seems to be a report of feelings, but it also involves a probability of action. We are disposed to do to a person we love the things he likes or loves to have done. We are not disposed to do to a person we dislike (or especially to a person we hate) the things he likes or loves to have done; on the contrary we are disposed to do the things he dislikes or hates to have done. With respect to a person with whom we interact, then, to "love" is to behave in ways having certain kinds of effects, possibly with accompanying conditions which may be felt.

WANTS, NEEDS, DESIRES, AND WISHES

Some mentalistic terms refer to conditions which affect both the susceptibility to reinforcement and the strength of already reinforced behavior. We use "want" to describe a shortage: a hungry man wants food in the simple sense that food is wanting. "Needs" originally meant violent force, restraint, or compulsion, and we still make a distinction between wanting to act (because of positively reinforcing consequences) and needing to act (because not acting will have aversive consequences), but for most purposes the terms are interchangeable. We say that a car needs gasoline and, much less idiomatically, that gasoline is wanting, but to say that a person "wants to get out" suggests aversive control. The significant fact is that a person who needs or wants food is particularly likely to be reinforced by food and that he is particularly likely to engage in any behavior which has previously been reinforced with food. A person under aversive control is particularly likely to be reinforced if he escapes and to engage in any behavior which has led to escape.

If we know the level of deprivation or aversive stimulation, we can more accurately predict how reinforcing a given event will be and how likely it is that a person will engage in relevant behavior. The knowledge has long been used for purposes of control. People have been made hungry so that they will "work for food" and so that they can be reinforced with food, as they have been made miserable so that they will act in ways which reduce their misery.

An event is not reinforcing *because* it reduces a need. Food is reinforcing even when it does not satiate, and deprivation can be changed in ways which are not reinforcing. The relation between a state of deprivation and the strength of appropriate behavior is presumably due to survival value. If behavior leading to ingestion were strong at all times, a person would grossly overeat and use his energies inefficiently.

It is a mistake to say that food is reinforcing *because* we feel hungry or *because* we feel the need for food, or that we are more likely to engage in food-reinforced behavior because we feel hungry. It is the *condition* felt as hunger which would have been selected in the evolution of the species as most immediately involved in operant reinforcement.

The states associated with wanting and needing are more likely to be felt if no relevant behavior is at the moment possible. The lover writes "I want you" or "I need you" when nothing else can be done, and if he is doing anything else, aside from writing, it must be a matter of existing in the state which he describes with these expressions. If behavior then becomes possible, it is easy to say that it was caused by the want or need, rather than by the deprivation or aversive stimulation responsible for both the behavior and the state felt.

Desiring, longing, hoping, and yearning are more closely related to a current absence of appropriate behavior because they terminate when action begins. "I miss you" could almost be thought of as a metaphor based on target practice, equivalent to "My behavior with respect to you as a person cannot reach its mark" or "I look for you and fail to find you." The lover in the arms of his beloved is not instantly free of wanting and needing her, but he is no longer missing her or longing or yearning for her. Wishing is perhaps most exclusively a reference to a heightened state of deprivation or aversive stimulation when no behavior is possible. A person may wish that he could act ("I wish I could go") or he may wish for the consequences ("I wish I were there").

The effects of operant reinforcement are often represented as inner states or possessions. When we reinforce a person we are said to give him a motive or incentive, but we infer the motive or the incentive from the behavior. We call a person highly motivated when all we know is that he behaves energetically.

Depriving a person of something he needs or wants is not a forceful act, and the effect builds up slowly, but states of deprivation are given a more dramatic role when they are called drives or urges. Freud saw men mercilessly "driven by powerful biological forces dwelling in the depths of the mind or personality." We are said to be at the mercy of sex, hunger, and hatred, even though they are said to supply the psychic energy needed for action. Freud's libido has been defined as "emotional or psychic energy derived from primitive biological urges." These metaphors are based on aversive control. The coachman does *drive* his horses by whipping them until they move forward, and, in the case of hunger at least, strong internal stimulation may have a similar function, but deprivation as such is not a driving force.

Mentalistic terms associated with reinforcers and with the states in which reinforcers are effective make it difficult to spot functional relations. For example, the statement "The term 'aggression' should be restricted to behavior motivated by the wish to injure" is intended to make a useful distinction between behavior which is merely aggressive in form and any part of such behavior which is emitted because it injures another person, but nothing is gained by speaking of the wish to injure or, in particular, of being motivated by a wish. When the Utilitarians held that pleasure and pain were the "motives influencing human behavior" they were referring to feelings associated with consequences rather than motives. The experimental analysis of contingencies of reinforcement puts these matters in better order.

IDEA AND WILL

The consequences which shape and maintain the behavior called an operant are not present in the setting in which a response occurs; they have become part of the history of the organism. The current setting may affect the probability of a response, as we shall see in the next chapter, but it is not the only thing that does so. To alter a probability is not to *elicit* a response, as in a reflex.

A person may feel or otherwise observe some of the conditions associated with the probability that he will behave in a given way. For example, he may say that he "feels like going," that he "wants to go," that he "should like to go," or that he "wishes to go." The same terms are used to identify reinforcers—as in saying, "I feel like a drink," "I want a drink," "I should like a drink," or "I wish I had a drink." It is possible that the report "I feel like going" is close to "I feel now as I have felt in the past when I have gone"; and "I want to go" may be a report of deprivation or a shortage. "I wish" is, as we have seen, probably closer to a report of a sheer probability of action. Whether or not a person feels or otherwise observes the likelihood of a response, the simple fact is that at some point a response occurs.

To distinguish an operant from an elicited reflex, we say that the operant response is "emitted." (It might be better to say simply that it appears, since emission may imply that behavior exists inside the organism and then comes out. But the word need not mean ejection; light is not in the hot filament before it is emitted.) The principal feature is that there seems to be no necessary prior causal event. We recognize this when we say that "it occurred to him to go" as if to say that "the act of going occurred to him." "Idea" is used to represent behavior in this sense (we say "the idea occurred to him"), but in expressions like "to get an idea," or "to borrow an idea" the word suggests an independent entity. Nevertheless, when we say, "I have an idea; let's try the rear door; it may be unlocked," what is "had" is the behavior of trying the rear door. When a person successfully imitates a dancing teacher, he may be said to "get the idea," although what he gets is nothing more than behavior similar to that of the teacher. Nor need we refer to more than behavior when we say that a person who laughs at a joke has "got the point," or that a person who responds appropriately to a passage in a book has "got its meaning."

The apparent lack of an immediate cause in operant behavior has led to the invention of an initiating event. Behavior is said to be put into play when a person wills to act. The term has a confusing history. The simple future, as in "He will go," takes on an additional meaning when we say, "He *will* go in spite of the danger." Willing is close to choosing, particularly when the choice is between acting or not acting; to will or to choose is evidently as unheralded as to act. By attributing otherwise unexplained behavior to an act of will or choice, one seems to resolve puzzlement. That is perhaps the principal *raison d'être* of the concept; behavior is satisfactorily accounted for as long as we have no reason to explain the act of will. But the conditions which determine the form of probability of an operant are in a person's history. Since they are not conspicuously represented in the current setting, they are easily overlooked. It is then easy to believe that the will is free and that the person is free to choose. The issue is determinism. The spontaneous generation of behavior has reached the same stage as the spontaneous generation of maggots and micro-organisms in Pasteur's day.

"Freedom" usually means the absence of restraint or coercion, but more comprehensively it means a lack of any prior determination: "All things that come to be, except acts of will, have causes." Some theologians have been concerned for the freedom needed in order to hold a person responsible, and they have not been so easily satisfied; so-called Arminian doctrine held that a person acts freely only if he has chosen to act and *only if the choosing to act was brought about by another instance of choosing*.

The conspicuousness of the causes is at issue when reflex behavior is called involuntary—one is not free to sneeze or not to sneeze; the initiating cause is the pepper. Operant behavior is called voluntary, but it is not really uncaused; the cause is simply harder to spot. The critical condition for the apparent exercise of free will is positive reinforcement, as the result of which a person feels free and calls himself free and say he does as he *likes* or what he *wants* or is *pleased* to do. (As we shall see in Chapter 12, a more important point is that positively reinforcing consequences do not generate avoidance or escape or any behavior designed to change the conditions in which it occurs.)

Like "idea," "will" is used almost interchangeably with behavior or at least with the probability of behaving. A willingness is a readiness or likelihood. A health authority has said that the important thing in maintaining a regimen of exercise or diet is will power; all he means is that the important thing is that a person continue to exercise or diet. A leader's "will to power" suggests behavior reinforced by economic, religious, or governmental accretions in power. The statement that "some people do not will because they are afraid" seems to refer to nothing more than the fact that they do not *behave* because they are afraid. The biographical statement that "the girl he was infatuated with [whom he never met] was a destructive agent, paralyzing his will" presumably means that she paralyzed some parts of his behavior.

A very different role of the will follows from its seeming spontaneity and mystery, which suggest that consequences may be produced without physical action. "It was with the magic of his own will that Brahma created whatever is." It is by an act of will that a person is supposed to influence the fall of dice in psychokinesis.

PURPOSE AND INTENTION

Possibly no charge is more often leveled against behaviorism or a science of behavior than that it cannot deal with purpose or intention. A stimulus-response formula has no answer, but operant behavior is the very field of purpose and intention. By its nature it is directed toward the future: a person acts *in order that* something will happen, and the order is temporal. "Purpose" was once commonly used as a verb, as we now use "propose." "I propose to go" is similar to "I intend to go." If instead we speak of our purpose or intention in going, it is easy to suppose that the nouns refer to things.

A good deal of misunderstanding has arisen from the fact that early representations of purpose were spatial. The racer's purpose is to reach the goal, and we play parcheesi with the purpose of bringing our pieces home. In the mazes in which purposive behavior was once studied, organisms moved toward the place where reinforcement was to occur. To use goal for purpose ("What is his goal in life?") is to identify it with a terminus. But it is meaningless, for example, to say that the goal—let alone the purpose—of life is death, even though the ultimate termination is death. One does not live in order to die or with the purpose of dying, whether we are speaking in terms of natural selection or operant conditioning.

Goals and purposes are confused in speaking of purpose in a homing device. A missile reaches its target when its course is appropriately controlled, in part by information coming from the target during its flight. Such a device is sometimes said to "have purpose built into it," but the feed-back used in guidance (the heart of cybernetics) is not reinforcement, and the missile has no purpose in the present sense. (Feedback may be used in a kind of explicit goal-seeking behavior to be discussed in Chapter 8.)

Not all consequences are reinforcing, and much of the effect of those which are depends upon the contingencies. Psychoanalysts have often said that the gambler's true pur-pose is to punish himself by losing. It is almost always the case that the gambler eventually loses, and the behavior therefore has that consequence, but it is not therefore rein-forcing. Gambling can be demonstrated in many other species and is explained by a special schedule of reinforce-ment to be noted in a moment. The ultimate loss (the "neg-ative utility") does not offset the effect of the schedule.

The Utilitarians supposed that it might be possible to measure quantities of pleasure and pain in such a way that the pleasure generated by socially objectionable behavior could be offset by a calculated amount of pain in the form of punishment. Unfortunately, the condition generated by a reinforcer and felt as pleasure is relatively insignificant in determining the quantity of behavior produced compared with the schedule of reinforcement.

A valid distinction lies back of the statement "Motives and purposes are in the brain and heart of man, whereas consequences are in the world of fact." Remove the gratui-tous physiologizing, and the point is made that motives and purposes are in people while contingencies of reinforcement are in the environment, but motives and purposes are at best the effects of reinforcements. The change wrought by reinforcement is often spoken of as "the acquisition of purpose or intention," and we are said to "give a person a purpose" by reinforcing him in a given way. These are convenient expressions, but the basic fact is that when a person is "aware of his purpose," he is feeling or observing introspectively a condition produced by reinforcement.

Seeking or looking for something seems to have a particularly strong orientation toward the future. We learn to look for an object when we acquire behavior which commonly has the consequence of discovering it. Thus, to look for a match is to look in a manner previously reinforced by finding matches. To seek help is to act in ways which have in the past led to help. If past consequences have not been very explicit, we are likely to look in vague and unproductive ways. People can usually say what they are looking for and why they are looking in a given place, but like other species they also may not be able to do so.

Many features of the debate about purpose in human behavior are reminiscent of the debate about purpose in evolution. As the *Columbia Encyclopedia* puts it:

> A still prevalent misunderstanding of evolution is the belief that an animal or plant changes in order to better adapt to its environment; e.g., that it develops an eye for the purpose of seeing. Since mutation is a random process and since most mutations are harmful rather than neutral or beneficial to the organism, it is evident that the occurrence of a variation is itself a matter of chance, and that one cannot speak of a will or purpose on the part of the individual to develop a new structure or trait that might prove helpful.

FEELINGS ASSOCIATED WITH SCHEDULES OF REINFORCEMENT

The probability that a person will respond in a given way because of a history of operant reinforcement changes as the contingencies change. Associated bodily conditions can be felt or observed introspectively, and they are often cited as the causes of the states or changes in probability.

When a given act is almost always reinforced, a person is said to have a feeling of confidence. A tennis player reports that he practices a particular shot "until he feels confident"; the basic fact is that he practices until a certain proportion of his shots are good. Frequent reinforcement also builds faith. A person feels sure, or certain, that he will be successful. He enjoys a sense of mastery, power, or potency. The infant is said to acquire a sense of infantile omnipotence. Frequent reinforcement also builds and maintains an interest in what a person is doing. In all this the behavior is erroneously attributed to the feelings rather than to the contingencies responsible for what is felt.

When reinforcement is no longer forthcoming, behavior undergoes "extinction" and appears rarely, if at all. A person is then said to suffer a loss of confidence, certainty, or sense of power. Instead, his feelings range from a lack of interest through disappointment, discouragement, and a sense of impotence to a possibly deep depression, and these feelings are then said—erroneously—to explain the absence of the behavior. For example, a person is said to be unable to go to work because he is discouraged or depressed, although his not going, together with what he feels, is due to a lack of reinforcement—either in his work or in some other part of his life.

Frustration is a rather different condition, which includes a tendency, often characteristic of a failure to be reinforced, to attack the system. Thus, a person who kicks the vending machine which has failed to deliver cigarettes or bawls out his wife who has forgotten to buy them is said to do so because of frustration. The expression "frustrated expectations" refers specifically to a condition produced by the termination of accustomed reinforcement.

A different kind of feeling is associated with the lack of

an appropriate occasion for behavior, the archetypal pattern of which is homesickness. When a person has left home for the first time, much of the behavior appropriate to that environment can no longer be emitted. The condition felt may be similar to depression, which is said to be common in people who have moved from one city to another. It is called "nostalgia"—literally, the pain generated by a strong tendency to return home when return is impossible. A similar condition prevails when one is simply lost, and the word is then "forlorn." A "lovelorn" person is unable to emit behavior directed toward the person he loves. A person who is "alone" may feel lonesome; the essential condition is that there is no one with whom he can talk or behave in other ways. The behavior of the homesick, forlorn, lovelorn, or lonely is commonly attributed to the feelings experienced rather than to the absence of a familiar environment.

Most reinforcements occur intermittently, and the schedules on which they are programmed generate conditions which are described with a wide range of terms. The so-called ratio schedules supply many good examples. When the ratio of responses to reinforcements is favorable, the behavior is commonly attributed to (1) diligence, industry, or ambition, (2) determination, stubbornness, staying power, or perseverance (continuing to respond over long periods of time without results), (3) excitement or enthusiasm, or (4) dedication or compulsion.

The ratio of responses to reinforcements may be "stretched" until it becomes quite unfavorable. This has happened in many incentive systems, such as the piece-rate pay of home industries in the nineteenth century. The schedule generates a dangerously high level of activity, and those interested in the welfare of workers usually oppose it. It is not unknown, however, in daily life. A writer who makes his living by writing one article or story after another is on a kind of fixed-ratio schedule, and he is often aware of one result: the completion of one article is often followed by a period resembling extinction during which he is unable to start a new one. The condition is sometimes called "abulia," defined as a lack of will power, or a neurotic inability to act, and this is often cited as the source of the trouble, in spite of the fact that the schedule produces a similar effect in a wide range of species.

Variable-ratio schedules, in which reinforcement occurs after a given average number of responses but in which the next response to be reinforced cannot be predicted, are particularly interesting. A favorable history in which the average is slowly enlarged is said to generate will power, together with large amounts of psychic energy, or libido. It is said that Hitler prolonged the Second World War for nearly a year "by an incredible exercise of will power which all the others in Germany lacked," but his behavior (and hence his "will power") can be plausibly attributed to an extraordinarily favorable program (favorable for Hitler, disastrous for the world) in which each of a series of reinforcing successes required an increasingly greater amount of effort. (This kind of interpretation of a historical event can never be more than plausible, but it is a better explanation than will power.)

All gambling systems are based on variable-ratio schedules of reinforcement, although their effects are usually attributed to feelings. It is frequently said, for example, that people gamble because of the excitement, but the excitement is clearly a collateral product. It is also sometimes said that people gamble "to satisfy their sense of mastery, to dominate, to win"—in spite of the fact that gamblers almost always eventually lose. The inconsistency is explained by calling the gambler who ruins himself and his family "compulsive" or "pathological," his "irrational" behavior thus being attributed to an illness. His behavior is "abnormal" in the sense that not everyone responds with similar dedication to the prevailing contingencies, but the fact is simply that not everyone has been exposed to a program through which a highly unfavorable ratio is made effective. The same variable-ratio schedule affects those who explore, prospect, invent, conduct scientific research, and compose works of art, music, or literature, and in these fields a high level of activity is usually attributed to dedication rather than compulsion or irrationality.

It is characteristic of intermittent reinforcement that behavior may be sustained over long periods of time with very little return. This has been explained by saying, "Human beings are creatures of hope and not genetically designed to resign themselves," but there is nothing essentially human about the effects, and it is not hope or resignation but the contingencies which are the conspicuous and accessible cause.

AVERSIVE STIMULI AND PUNISHMENT

Aversive stimuli, which generate a host of bodily conditions felt or introspectively observed, are the stimuli which function as reinforcers when they are reduced or terminated. They have different effects when related to behavior in other ways. In respondent conditioning, if a previously neutral stimulus, such as a bell, is frequently followed after an interval by a noxious stimulus, such as an electric shock, the bell comes to elicit reactions, primarily in the autonomic nervous system, which are felt as anxiety. The bell has become a conditioned aversive stimulus, which may then have the effect of changing the probability of any positively reinforced behavior in progress. Thus, a person engaged in a lively conversation may begin to speak less energetically or more erratically or may stop speaking altogether at the approach of someone who has treated him aversively. On the other hand, his negatively reinforced behavior may be strengthened, and he may act more compulsively or aggressively or move to escape. His behavior does not change because he feels anxious; it changes because of the aversive contingencies which generate the condition felt as anxiety. The change in feeling and the change in behavior have a common cause.

Punishment is easily confused with negative reinforcement, sometimes called "aversive control." The same stimuli are used, and negative reinforcement might be defined as the punishment of not behaving, but punishment is designed to remove behavior from a repertoire, whereas negative reinforcement generates behavior.

Punishing contingencies are just the reverse of reinforcing. When a person spanks a child or threatens to spank him because he has misbehaved, he is *presenting* a negative reinforcer rather than removing one, and when a government fines an offender or puts him in prison, it is removing a positive reinforcer or a situation in which behavior may be positively reinforced rather than presenting a negative one. If the effect were simply the reverse of the effect of reinforcement, a great deal of behavior could be easily explained; but when behavior is punished, various stimuli generated by the behavior or the occasion are conditioned in the respondent pattern, and the punished behavior is then displaced by incompatible behavior conditioned as escape or avoidance. A punished person remains "inclined" to behave in a punishable way, but he avoids punishment by doing something else instead, possibly nothing more than stubbornly doing nothing.

What a person feels when he is in a situation in which he has been punished or when he has engaged in previously punished behavior depends upon the type of punishment, and this often depends in turn upon the punishing agent or institution. If he has been punished by his peers, he is said to feel shame; if he has been punished by a religious agency, he is said to feel a sense of sin; and if he has been punished by a governmental agency, he is said to feel guilt. If he acts to avoid further punishment, he may moderate the condition felt as shame, sin, or guilt, but he does not act because of his feelings or because his feelings are then changed; he acts because of the punishing contingencies to which he has been exposed.

The condition felt as shame, guilt, or a sense of sin is not due simply to an earlier occurrence of an aversive stimulus. A thunderstorm may set up conditions felt as anxiety, and during a storm positively reinforced behavior may be weakened, and negatively reinforced (such as flight or concealment) strengthened, but this condition is not felt as guilt. The point has been made by saying that "a person cannot feel guilty if he has no object-directed impulses to feel guilty about." More exactly, he feels guilty only when he behaves, or tends to behave, in a punishable way.

A writer who says, "The more I read of the early and mid-Victorians, the more I see anxiety and worry as the leading clue to understanding them," is suggesting an explanation of behavior in terms of feelings generated by punishing circumstances, where the feelings are inferred from the behavior they are used to explain. He is not claiming to have any direct information about feelings, and presumably means understanding what they said and did, but anxiety and worry are useful clues only if they can be explained in turn. The writer attempts to do this when he continues: "They were trying to hold together incompatible opposites, and they worried because they failed. . . . They worried about immortality, they worried about sex, they worried about politics and money." These were the external circumstances responsible for their behavior and for the conditions felt as worry.

The frequency, severity, and schedule of punishment generate other aspects of behavior often attributed to feelings or traits of character. In many familiar instances, behavior has both punishing and reinforcing consequences. If behavior still occurs but in a weakened form, it may be said to show inhibition, timidity, embarrassment, fear, or caution. Excessive punishment is said to make a shortage of positive reinforcement more critical and leave a person "more vulnerable to severe depression and to giving up." We treat what is felt not by changing the feelings but by changing the contingencies—for example, by evoking the behavior without punishing it, so that conditioned aversive stimuli may undergo extinction.

Behavior which is strong in spite of punishing consequences is said to show bravery, courage, or possibly audacity. We encourage a person not by making him feel more courageous but by emphasizing reinforcing consequences and minimizing punishing. A fool rushes into a dangerous situation not because he feels reckless but because reinforcing consequences have completely offset punishing; and we may attempt to correct his behavior by supplying other (possibly verbal) punishments.

When punishment is particularly severe, the self-knowledge discussed in Chapter 2 may be affected. The behavior suppressed may include the behavior involved in knowing about associated bodily conditions. The result is what Freud called "repression." For Freud, however, the process involved feelings rather than behavior, and it took place in the depths of the mind. Feelings were repressed by other feelings and policed by a censor from whom they sometimes escaped in devious ways. They could continue to be troublesome, however, and man was said to be "haunted by his repressed longings." I shall discuss some behavioral aspects later.

STRUCTURALISM

Early studies of behavior were often said to confine themselves to form or structure—to treat behavior, for example, as nothing more than "muscle twitches." The refusal to accept feelings and states of mind as causes and an abiding concern for "objectivity" seemed to support such a view. Habit formation was a structuralist principle: to acquire a habit was merely to become accustomed to behaving in a given way. The contingencies of reinforcement which generated the behavior, like the contingencies of survival which produced an instinct, were neglected.

Frequency theories of learning were also structural. They asserted simply that what has happened once will happen again, that an organism will tend to do what it has done most often in the past. As I have noted, behavioralism confined itself to the topography of political behavior, and structuralism in anthropology is often not far beyond the position that customs are followed simply because it is customary to follow them. Early Greek and Persian justice was simple and swift because it was based entirely on the topography of a crime: a person who killed another was guilty of murder regardless of the circumstances. I shall note later the significance of the fact that support for the structuralist position has come from both phenomenology and existentialism, with their neglect of past and future in the search for the essential features of the here and now.

If behaviorism had not replaced the feelings and states of mind which it discarded as explanations, it could indeed be called a kind of structuralism, but it found replacements in the environment. As we learn more about the role of contingencies of reinforcement, we are more likely to move beyond formal properties. The point may be illustrated with the concept of imitation. In a purely formalistic definition, one organism might be said to be imitating another when it behaves as the other behaves, but, as we saw in Chapter 3, contingencies of both survival and reinforcement must be considered. The patrons of a restaurant are behaving in roughly the same way with respect to their dinners, but they are not imitating each other; they are behaving in similar ways because they are exposed to similar contingencies. The man who runs after a thief is not imitating him, though both are running.

Structuralism is involved in the distinction often drawn

between learning or competence and performance. The distinction was useful in early studies of learning because the changes in performance then observed were rather erratic. Since it was assumed that learning was an orderly process, there appeared to be a discrepancy, but it was resolved by supposing that learning was not very accurately revealed in the behavior the organism displayed. Performance was clearly a structuralist term; it referred to what an organism did without referring to why it did it. Improved techniques have revealed an orderly relation between performance and contingencies and have eliminated the need to appeal to a separate inner learning process or to competence.

The same confusion may be seen in the contention that operant and respondent conditioning represent a single process, a contention said to be opposed to the view that the two kinds of conditioning affect different systems of behavior, respondent conditioning being appropriate to the autonomic nervous system and operant conditioning to the skeletal musculature. It is true that much of the activity of the autonomic nervous system does not have natural consequences which could easily have become part of operant contingencies, but such consequences can be arranged. (In Chapter 11 I shall report an effort to bring the vascular system of the arm under operant control by instrumentally amplifying a measure of the volume of the arm.) But the basic difference is not in the topography of response systems but in the contingencies. The environmental arrangements which produce a conditioned reflex are quite different from those which produce operant behavior, regardless of the respective systems. (The fact that both processes may go on in a given situation also does not mean that they are the same process. A child acquiring operant behavior no doubt also acquires conditioned reflexes, and Pavlov's dog, though restrained by the experimental stand, was operantly reinforced in adventitious ways by the occasional presentation of food.) We must wait to see what learning processes the physiologist will eventually discover through direct observation, rather than through inferences; meanwhile, the contingencies permit a useful and important distinction.

Structuralism often goes beyond mere description, and one of its strategies has had a very long history. When the notion of a functional relation was not yet fully understood, explanations of phenomena were sought in their structures. Plato's doctrine of forms was an effort to explain events with principles derived from the same or similar events. It has been said that from Plato to Kepler mathematics was not regarded as describing celestial motion but as explaining it. The search for explanation in form or structure goes on. Gestalt psychology tried to supplement the structural notion of habit formation with organizational principles. Mathematical properties hold their old explanatory force; it has been said, for example, that for one anthropologist "the relations of kinship do not evolve as much as they tend to express algebraic relations."

As I noted in Chapter 1, a merely structural account may be supplemented by invoking time as an independent variable. The growth of the embryo from a fertilized egg to a fetus at term is a remarkable example of development, and it has been suggested that similar sequences in the growth "of a skill, of an art, of a concept in the mind" may be important. The behavior of a person or a culture is said to pass through various stages until it reaches maturity. The psychopathology of the drug addict has been said to be due to "arrested infantile psychic development." As these examples suggest, what grows is said to be something in the mind, as with Piaget, or in the personality, as with Freud. But if a child no longer behaves as he behaved a year before, it is not only because he has grown but because he has had the time to acquire a much bigger repertoire through exposure to new contingencies of reinforcement, and particularly because the contingencies affecting children at different ages are different. A child's world "develops," too.

Compared with the experimental analysis of behavior, developmental psychology stands in the position of evolutionary theory before Darwin. By the early nineteenth century it was well known that species had undergone progressive changes toward more adaptive forms. They were developing or maturing, and improved adaptation to the environment suggested a kind of purpose. The question was not whether evolutionary changes occurred but why. Both Lamarck and Buffon appealed to the purpose supposedly shown by the individual in adapting to his environment—a purpose somehow transmitted to the species. It remained for Darwin to discover the selective action of the environment, as it remains for us to supplement developmentalism in behavioral science with an analysis of the selective action of the environment.

THE MIND IN OPERANT BEHAVIOR

In most of this chapter I have been concerned with feelings or states of mind which may be interpreted as collateral products of the contingencies which generate behavior. It remains for us to consider other mentalistic processes, which are said to be needed if operant conditioning is to take place. The mind is not merely a spectator; it is said to play an active role in the determination of behavior.

Many English idioms containing the word "mind" suggest a probability of action, as in "I have a mind to go." Mind is often represented as an agent, scarcely to be distinguished from the person who has the mind. "It crossed my *mind* that I should go" is scarcely more than "It occurred to *me* that I should go." When responses of glands or smooth muscle (under control of the autonomic nervous system) are brought under operant control by making reinforcement contingent upon them, the result is said to demonstrate the control of "mind over matter"; but what it demonstrates is that a person may respond with his glands or his smooth

muscles under operant contingencies. A mechanical arm designed to be operated by muscles normally operating some
other part of the body is said to be "thought-operated" or
"operated by the mind," although it is operated by the person who originally moved some other part of his body.
When people shoot other people, it is said that "minds kill,
not guns," and that "a man's mind was the instrument directly responsible for the assassination of John F. Kennedy
and Martin Luther King," but people are shot by people,
not by minds.

The view that mental activity is essential to operant behavior is an example of the view that feelings or introspectively observed states are causally effective. When a person
replies to the question "Will you go tomorrow?" by saying,
"I don't know, I never know how I will feel," the assumption is that what is in doubt is the feeling rather than the behavior—that the person will go if he feels like going rather
than that he will feel like going if he goes. Neither statement
is, of course, an explanation.

There are other words referring to mental activites said
to be more specifically required by behavior. People must
"judge" what will or will not occur if they do or do not act
in certain ways. The dog in the Pavlovian experiment sali-
vates in anticipation of food or because it "expects" food.
In operant experiments a rat presses a lever because it "an-
ticipates" that food will be delivered or expects food to be
delivered when it does so. "In social learning theory the potential of the occurrence of a behavior is considered to be a
function of the expectancy that the behavior will lead to a
particular reinforcement or reinforcements and the value of
these reinforcements in a given situation." We should have
to translate these statements in some such way as this: "The
probability of behavior depends upon the kind or frequency
of reinforcement in similar situations in the past." A person
may well feel conditions associated with "judging," "antic-
ipating," and "expecting," but he does not need to do so.

Operant behavior is also said to require the "association" of ideas. The fact that a baby learns to avoid a hot stove is said to imply that "the baby has the ability to associate his act . . . with getting burned." But, as in a conditioned reflex, touching and burning are associated in the contingencies. Reinforcement is also said to "supply information": "With other than very young children we can never say that the major effect of reinforcement is other than a source of information used by the child to confirm or change his expectations and to develop new and tentative solutions." Increasing the probability that people will respond in certain ways is sometimes said to be a matter of "raising consciousness." How fast a rat will run in a maze is said to depend upon whether it "knows that food is any longer available in the end box." I shall return to knowledge, information, and consciousness in later chapters.

Another supposed mental process said to be needed in operant conditioning is understanding. People must "understand the regularities upon which they can count." Their action must be "grounded on the understanding of how things behave." Another state said to be needed is belief. People must believe that what they are doing has some chance of obtaining what they want or avoiding something to which they are averse. But the chances are in the contingencies. The relation of beliefs to other conditions, such as wants and needs, can be easily stated: to say that "desires enter into the causation of beliefs" is simply to say that the probability of behavior with which a belief is associated depends not only upon reinforcement but upon a state of deprivation or aversive stimulation.

It is sometimes said that operant conditioning is simply one aspect of the pursuit of happiness, and the expression will help to summarize several points in this chapter. Happiness is a feeling, a by-product of operant reinforcement. The things which make us happy are the things which reinforce us, but it is the things, not the feelings, which must be identified and used in prediction, control, and interpretation. Pursuit suggests purpose: we act to achieve happiness. But pursuit, like search, is simply behavior which has been reinforced by achieving something. Behavior becomes pursuit only after reinforcement. It has been said that the pursuit of happiness cannot be an explanation of behavior because "nothing proves that men in modern societies are happier than men in archaic societies," but operant reinforcement is effective quite apart from any ultimate gain, as the negative utility of gambling abundantly demonstrates.

5

Perceiving

Perhaps the most difficult problem faced by behaviorism has been the treatment of conscious content. Are we not all familiar with colors, sounds, tastes, and smells which have no counterparts in the physical world? What is their place in a behavioristic account? I believe the answer is to be found in the special role assigned to stimuli in an operant analysis. It calls for a certain amount of technical detail, and I shall treat it in some depth.

PERCEIVER OR RECEIVER?

In the traditional view a person responds to the world around him in the sense of acting upon it. Etymologically, to experience the world is to test it, and to perceive it is to capture it—to take it in and possess it. For the Greeks, to know was to be intimate with. A person could not, of course, capture and possess the real world, but he could make copies of it, and these were the so-called data—the givens—

with which, in lieu of reality, he worked. He could store them in his memory and later retrieve and act upon them more or less as he might have done when they were first given.

The opposing view—common, I believe, to all versions of behaviorism—is that the initiating action is taken by the environment rather than by the perceiver. The reflex was a conspicuous example, and a stimulus-response version of behaviorism kept to the same pattern, as did information theory and some computer models. A part of the environment entered the body, was transformed there, perhaps was stored, and eventually emerged as a response. Curiously enough, this differed from the mentalistic picture only with respect to the initiator of action. In both theories the environment penetrated the body: in the mentalistic view, it was taken in by the perceiver; in the stimulus-response view, it battered its way in. The two formulations could be combined—"an image of the outer world striking the retina of the eye activates a most intricate process that results in vision: the transformation of the retinal image into a perception." Both formulations directed attention to the inner representation of reality in its various transformations. A basic question could be put this way: What becomes of the stimulus?

In an operant analysis, and in the radical behaviorism built upon it, *the environment stays where it is and where it has always been—outside the body.*

THE STIMULUS CONTROL
OF OPERANT BEHAVIOR

The environment affects an organism after, as well as before, it responds. To stimulus and response we add consequence, and it is not just a third term in a sequence. The occasion upon which behavior occurs, the behavior itself, and its consequences are interrelated in the contingencies of reinforcement we have already examined. As the result of its place in these contingencies, a stimulus present when a response is reinforced acquires some control over the response. It does not then elicit the response as in a reflex; it simply makes it more probable that it will occur again, and it may do so in combination with other conditions affecting probability, such as those discussed in the preceding chapter. A response reinforced upon a given occasion is most likely to occur on a very similar occasion, but because of a process called generalization it may appear on occasions sharing only some of the same properties. If, however, it is reinforced only when a particular property is present, that property acquires exclusive control through a process called discrimination.

The role of the stimulus gives operant behavior a special character. The behavior is not dominated by the current setting, as it appeared to be in stimulus-response psychology; it is not "stimulus-bound." Nevertheless, the environmental *history* is still in control; the genetic endowment of the species plus the contingencies to which the individual has been exposed still determine what he will perceive.

CONDITIONS AFFECTING WHAT IS SEEN

Many of the issues discussed in the preceding chapter extend to the stimulus control of operant behavior. For example, perception is in a sense purposive or intentional. A person is not an indifferent spectator soaking up the world like a sponge. An early objection to John Locke's theory of human understanding was that stimulation seemed to be coldly engraved on the *tabula rasa* of the mind, and efforts were made to supplement the theory by saying that a person "beheld things as liked or disliked, approved or disapproved, or pleasing or displeasing," or that a person "judged" the world as he perceived it. But expressions of that sort simply assign to fanciful inner processes what is to be found in genetic endowment and personal history. We are not merely "mindful" of the world about us; we respond to it in idiosyncratic ways because of what has happened when we have been in contact with it. And just as operant conditioning does not mean that a person "infers what will happen when he acts," so the control exerted by stimuli does not mean that he "infers what exists in the world around him."

It is often pointed out that a person who has been driven over a route as a passenger cannot find his way as well as one who has himself driven the route an equal number of times. Animals carried about in a given setting do not then move about in it as well as animals who have already moved about. Both have been exposed to the same visual stimuli, but the contingencies have been different. To ask why the passenger and the animal carried about have not "acquired knowledge of the setting" is to miss the point. They have not acquired behavior under the control of the setting.

When a stimulus is weak or vague, it is often clear that other conditions are affecting the probability that a person will see a thing in a given way. The lover "thinks he sees" his beloved in a crowd but only if the visual stimulus is fleeting or obscure. (The effect is studied in the laboratory by exposing a stimulus for a very short time, say, or near the edge of the visual field, or in faint light.) A slight noise at night is heard as a burglar or a mouse by those who respond vigorously to burglars or mice. Level of deprivation makes a difference; one mistakenly "hears the telephone" if a call is important, and the sexually deprived see phalluses or vaginas in objects bearing little geometrical similarity to those organs. In other words, a person sees one thing *as something else* when the probability of seeing the latter is high and the control exerted by the former is low.

The importance of the history of the perceiver is clear when a chess master looks at a game in progress. What he sees is very different from what is seen by one who does not play chess or who has not played it long. For the master, the setting is an occasion upon which many different moves have been made with good or bad results in games with which he is familiar. To the person who is just learning to play, the setting may be an occasion for a number of moves but moves which have not been much affected by consequences. To the completely naïve, the board and its pieces are a visual setting to be described only through possible resemblances to situations in his non-chess-playing history.

We recognize the importance of a history of reinforcement when we undertake to make it more likely that a person will see a particular thing—or, in other words, that he will engage in a particular kind of seeing. We can present a thing suddenly or conspicuously or in a novel and hence surprising way, and we can point to it if our subject has learned to follow a point—that is, if he has learned to behave effectively under contingencies in which a thing indicated plays an important part. But we can also arrange that a particular object will be seen by establishing contingencies which can be met only by responding to it. Traffic signs are designed to be easily seen, but we see them or ignore them largely because of the contingent consequences. Measures of this sort are often said to increase a person's awareness, or to expand his mind or consciousness, but they simply bring him under more effective control of his environment.

The structuralists have tried to explain perception in terms of the form, or configuration, of what is perceived. Gestalt psychologists may be said to have argued that certain kinds of patterns force the organism to perceive them in certain ways. Some illusions, for example, seem irresistible; we see what we know is not really there. Some examples seem to be reasonably explained in terms of natural selection: it is not surprising that when we see a bird fly behind a tree trunk, we behave as if it continued to exist when out of sight, and even see it move from one side to the other as we see a traffic light jump from red to green.

Small gaps in orderly patterns are neglected with profit as we "neglect" the blind spots in our eyes. We do not need to postulate structural principles to explain these characteristics. Contingencies of reinforcement also contribute to irresistible perceptions: a rotating trapezoid which refuses to appear to go around is made more effective by representing it as a window frame.

EXPERIENCE VERSUS REALITY

The great differences in what is seen at different times in a given setting suggest that a stimulus cannot be described in purely physical terms. Behaviorism is said to be at fault in failing to recognize that what is important is "how the situation looks to a person" or "how a person interprets a situation" or "what meaning a situation has for a person." But to investigate how a situation looks to a person, or how he interprets it, or what meaning it has for him, we must examine his behavior with respect to it, including his descriptions of it, and we can do this only in terms of his genetic and environmental histories. To explain how the real world is converted into an internal iconic representation, one authority has suggested the following: "For perception to go beyond the evidence of the senses the brain must have stored information, allowing it to use available sensory data to choose between possibilities derived from past situations. Behavior is not controlled directly by stimuli . . . but by the brain's hypotheses of what probably lies in outside space and in the immediate future." (This is an example, by the way, of a current practice of avoiding dualism by substituting "brain" for "mind." The brain is said to use data, make hypotheses, make choices, and so on, as the mind was once said to have done. In a behavioristic account it is the person who does these things.) But we observe simply that a person responds to a current setting ("the evidence of his senses") because of his exposure to contingencies of which the setting has been a part. We have no reason to say that he has stored information which he now retrieves in order to interpret the evidence of his senses.

Some of the history relevant to perception may have occurred during the evolution of the species. What is seen seems to "depart from the object world," for example, in the illusions mentioned above, in some of which the mind is said to "infer and predict reality from incomplete data," but we should say instead that because of his genetic endowment a person responds in a possibly effective way to what seem to be fragmentary stimuli.

The psychophysicists have most rigorously explored the correspondence between experience and reality. Early psychologists, like Wundt and Titchener, tried to discover what a person saw (or heard, felt, and so on) under the pure control of current stimuli, free of the effects of previous exposure. A trained observer was to describe his sensations without making the "stimulus error"—that is, to describe what he was looking at as if he had never seen it before or could never have learned anything about it. He was to see a "patch of color" rather than an object; he was to have a salty taste rather than taste salt; he was to feel warm rather than the warmth of the sun on his skin.

In doing so, he was to see the irreducible elements of mental life, but even so, sensation seemed different from reality because changes in stimuli did not produce comparable changes in what was seen. A psychophysical function was said to represent the relation between the two worlds; but we could say instead that it represents facts about the discriminative control of stimuli. The position of conscious content grew weaker when methodological behaviorism, together with operationism and logical positivism, questioned the usefulness of sensations as scientific data, and psychophysicists then turned to the process of discrimination, as we have seen. But it was possible to study discrimination while believing in the existence of a world of experience.

Further studies of discrimination, particularly research on the sensory processes of animals, were responsible for further progress. In 1865 Claude Bernard had contended that "experimental studies of sense organs must be made on man because animals cannot directly account to us for the sensations they experience," but there is now an elaborate "animal psychophysics," in which stimulus control is analyzed with great precision. It is still likely to be said that the experimenter has "taught the animal to report what it sees," but the results can be much more consistently formulated in terms of the control set up by specific contingencies of reinforcement. Of all the great mentalistic explanations, the "understanding" or "knowledge" of the British empiricists has suffered the most ignominious fate: it has been reduced to the physiology of the eye and ear.

The distinction between a physical and a mental world, most often found in Western cultures, presumably arose, as in Plato's supposed discovery of the mind, in the effort to solve the dimensional problem of mental life; there was not enough room in the body for the copies of the world a person seemed to possess. Later, with the rise of science, a different kind of discrepancy appeared. Were the qualities of images and ideas to be found in nature at all? To use a well-worn example, did a falling tree make a noise if no one heard it? Light might be a matter of corpuscles or waves, but it certainly did not seem to be a matter of colors; green was not a wave length of light. This was not a serious problem for early philosophers, who had no reason to question the fact that they lived in a world of colors, sounds, and so on. Nor is it a problem to millions of people today, who also believe that they do so. Nor is it a problem for a behaviorist.

To argue that layman and scientist are simply looking at two *aspects* of the same thing is to miss the point, because aspect is what causes trouble: people see different things when they have been exposed to different contingencies of reinforcement. Like everyone else, the scientist sees green, but he also responds in other ways to the same setting. It is a mistake, however, to say that the concepts of science are constructed from personal sensory experience. Both layman and scientist respond—in similar or different ways, depending upon the contingencies—to the features of a given setting. (I shall return to the personal knowledge of the scientist in Chapter 9.)

The stimulus control of behavior is subject to severe limitations. Our genetic endowment restricts control to electromagnetic radiation in the visible range, for example, and to sonic sounds, and even within these ranges the eye and ear have their defects. Their faults are not, however, a matter of faulty inferences. The discrepancies are not in a correspondence between experience and reality but in stimulus control.

It is easier to make the point when reality is more complex. When an unfortunate war is attributed to "misperception" or a seminar is devoted to the "discrepancy between the reality and perception of technological change," translation is mandatory. How are we to perceive the reality of the war or the technological change in order to discover that it has indeed been misperceived? We are always "dealing with reality," although the term must be taken to include more than a current presentation. The important differences are among behaviors, and these in turn are explained by differences in past contingencies.

THE COPY THEORY

Those who believe that we see copies of the world may contend that we never see the world itself, but it is at least equally plausible to say that we never see anything else. The copy theory of perception is most convincing with respect to visual stimuli. They are frequently copied in works of art as well as in optical systems of mirrors and lenses, and hence it is not difficult to imagine some plausible system of storage. It is much less convincing to say that we do not hear the sounds made by an orchestra but rather some inner reproduction. Music has temporal patterns, and only recently have copies been available which might lend themselves to a mental metaphor. The argument is wholly unconvincing in the field of taste and odor, where it is not easy to imagine copies distinguishable from the real thing, and it is seldom if ever made in the case of feeling. When we feel the texture of a sheet of paper, we feel the paper, not some internal representation. Possibly we do not need copies of tastes, odors, and feelings, since we are already physically intimate with them, and for presumably the same reason we are said to feel internal states like hunger or anger rather than copies.

The trouble is that the notion of an inner copy makes no progress whatsoever in explaining either sensory control or the psychology or physiology of perception. The basic difficulty was formulated by Theophrastus more than two thousand years ago:

> . . . with regard to hearing, it is strange of him [Empedocles] to imagine that he has really explained how creatures hear, when he has ascribed the process to internal sounds and assumed that the ear produces a sound within, like a bell. By means of this internal sound we might hear sounds without, but how should we hear this internal sound itself? The old problem would still confront us.

Similarly, as a modern authority has pointed out, it is as difficult to explain how we see a picture in the occipital cortex of the brain as to explain how we see the outside world, which it is said to represent. The *behavior* of seeing is neglected in all such formulations. It can take its proper place only if attention is given to other terms in the contingencies responsible for stimulus control.

SEEING IN THE ABSENCE OF THE THING SEEN

When a person recalls something he once saw, or engages in fantasy, or dreams a dream, surely he is not under the control of a current stimulus. Is he not then seeing a copy? Again, we must turn to his environmental history for an answer. After hearing a piece of music several times, a person may hear it when it is not being played, though probably not as richly or as clearly. So far as we know, he is simply doing in the absence of the music some of the things he did in its presence. Similarly, when a person sees a person or place in his imagination, he may simply be doing what he does in the presence of the person or place. Both "reminiscing" and "remembering" once meant "being mindful of again" or "bringing again to mind"—in other words, seeing again as one once saw. Explicit techniques of "calling to mind" are techniques of strengthening perceptual behavior, as we shall see in Chapter 7.

Behaviorism has been accused of "relegating one of the paramount concerns of the earlier psychologists—the study of the image—to a position of not just neglect, but disgrace." I believe, on the contrary, that it offers the only way in which the subject of imaging or imagining can be put in good order.

Seeing in the absence of the thing seen is familiar to almost everyone, but the traditional formulation is a metaphor. We tend to act to produce stimuli which are reinforcing when seen. If we have found the city of Venice reinforcing (we refer to one reinforcing effect when we call it beautiful), we may go to Venice in order to be thus reinforced. If we cannot go, we may buy pictures of Venice—realistic pictures in color of its most beautiful aspects, although a black-and-white sketch may be enough. Or we may see Venice by reading about it if we have acquired the capacity to visualize while reading. (Technology has made it much easier to see reinforcing things in their presence and hence has reduced the chance to see them in their absence. Two or three generations ago a child read, or was read to, from books with few or no illustrations; today he watches television or reads books with colored pictures on every page, and he is therefore much less likely to acquire a repertoire of seeing under the control of verbal stimuli.) With no external support whatsoever, we may simply "see Venice" because we are reinforced when we do so. We say that we daydream about Venice. The mistake is to suppose that because we create physical stimuli which enable us to see Venice more effectively by going to Venice or buying a picture, we must therefore create *mental* stimuli to be seen in memory. All we need to say is that if we are reinforced for seeing Venice, we are likely to engage in that behavior —that is, the behavior of seeing Venice—even when there is very little in the immediate setting which bears a resemblance to the city. According to one dictionary, fantasy is defined as "the act or function of forming images or representations in direct perception or in memory," but we could say as well that it is the act or function of seeing in direct perception or in memory.

We may also see a thing in its absence, not because we are immediately reinforced when we do so, but because we are then able to engage in behavior which is subsequently reinforced. Thus, we may see Venice in order to tell a friend how to find his way to a particular part of the city. If we were together in the city itself, we might take him along a given route, but we can "take ourselves along the route visually" when we are not there and describe it to him. We can do so more effectively by pointing to a map or a sketch of the route, but we do not consult a "cognitive map" when we describe what we see in "calling the city to mind." Knowing a city means possessing the behavior of getting about in it; it does not mean possessing a map to be followed in getting about. One may construct such a map from the actual city or by seeing the city when absent from it, but visualizing a route through a city in order to describe it to a friend is seeing *as* (not *what*) one sees in going through the city.

Claude Bernard might also have said that it is impossible to get animals to report the things they are imagining, but there is no reason why the contingencies under which a person sees things which are not there should not be effective with other species. It is possible to get animals to respond to after-images, and by increasing deprivation we can induce a pigeon to respond to a square "as if it were a triangle." There is no reason why, with such measures, we could not get it to respond to a blank surface when it has previously been reinforced only when the surface had a triangle projected upon it. The design of "verbal" contingencies which would permit it to tell us that it "saw" a triangle would be an interesting exercise.

A person is changed by the contingencies of reinforcement under which he behaves; he does not store the contingencies. In particular, he does not store copies of the stimuli which have played a part in the contingencies. There are no "iconic representations" in his mind; there are no "data structures stored in his memory"; he has no "cognitive map" of the world in which he has lived. He has simply been changed in such a way that stimuli now control particular kinds of perceptual behavior.

Seeing in the absence of the thing seen is most dramatically exemplified in dreaming when asleep. Current stimulation is then minimally in control, and a person's history and resulting states of deprivation and emotion get their chance. Freud emphasized the significance of wishes and fears plausibly inferred from dreaming, but unfortunately he was responsible for emphasizing the distinction between seeing and what is seen. The dreamer engaged in dream work; he staged the dream as a theatrical producer stages a play and then took his place in the audience and watched it. But dreaming is perceptual *behavior,* and the difference between behavior when asleep and when awake, either in or out of a relevant setting, is simply a difference in the controlling conditions.

Rapid eye movements during sleep seem to confirm this interpretation. When most actively dreaming, people move their eyes about as if they were observing a visual presentation. (The middle-ear muscles also seem to move during dreams involving auditory perception.) It has been argued that eye movement, as well as ear-muscle movement, show that "physiological input" affects dreaming, but such behavior is quite clearly a physiological *output.* We can scarcely suppose that the iconic representations observed in dreaming are under the eyelids or in the outer ear.

There are many ways of getting a person to see when there is nothing to be seen, and they can all be analyzed as the arrangement of contingencies which strengthen perceptual behavior. Certain practices in behavior therapy, in which the patient is asked to imagine various conditions or events, have been criticized as not genuinely behavioral because they make use of images. But there are no images in the sense of private copies, there is perceptual behavior; and the measures taken by the psychotherapist are designed to strengthen it. A change takes place in the patient's behavior if what he sees (hears, feels, and so on) has the same positively or negatively reinforcing effect as if he were seeing the things themselves. It is seldom if ever enough simply to instruct the patient to "have feelings," to ask him to feel sexually excited or nauseated, but he may be shown pornographic or nauseating material or be asked to "visualize as clearly as possible" a sexual or disgusting episode.

That a person may see things when there is nothing to be seen must have been a strong reason why the world of the mind was invented. It was hard enough to imagine how a copy of the current environment could get into the head where it could be "known," but there was at least a world outside which might account for it. But pure images seem to indicate a pure mind stuff. It is only when we ask how either the world or a copy of the world is seen that we lose interest in copies. Seeing does not require a thing seen.

MIND AND STIMULUS CONTROL

We saw in Chapter 4 that the word "mind" is sometimes a mere synonym for the person who acts. It can also stand for the person who perceives. When a person is out of touch with reality, his mind is said to be wandering, or possibly absent. The verb "to mind" often means simply to respond. We warn someone to mind the low ceiling, meaning simply that he should see and respond to it. In this sense we ask someone to mind the children, and he may complain that the children do not mind him.

Mind is also sometimes simply the place in which things are seen. Things "come to mind" or are "called to mind," and one who is suffering a delusion may be told that "it's all in your mind," as distinct from being in the real world. As the place in which things are perceived, mind is closely associated with copy theory and was an important part of the psychology of conscious content. When operationism led to the study of the process of discrimination rather than of sensations, a person was regarded as looking at or listening to the real world. He was no longer reporting his perceptions or sensations; he was reporting stimuli. The world was back where it belonged.

The issue is critical when we turn to the difference between seeing a thing and seeing that one is seeing it. If there are no copies of things inside the body at any time, then all that can be seen introspectively is the act of seeing, and this is what one reports when asked, "Do you see that?" It is still possible, however, to discriminate between things which are there or not there to be seen. I could be said to know that this sheet of paper is really there because I pick up a pen and write on it, and that the bright after-image which bothers me is not there because I do not try to brush it away. I have learned the difference between two kinds of seeing. The thirsty man does not reach for the fantasied glass of water, but the dreamer does not know that what he is seeing is "not really there," and he responds as fully as a person who is asleep can. (Introspective knowledge of dreaming is weak or lacking because the conditions needed for self-observation are lacking, and when such self-knowledge survives into the waking state, it usually disappears quickly as one forgets one's dreams.) It is also possible to know that you have seen something before. We re-cognize what we have once cognized. In a *déjà vu* this feature of self-knowledge is defective.

Other kinds of self-knowledge about stimulus control become available when we analyze the contingencies which control our behavior.

Verbal Behavior

Relatively late in its history, the human species underwent a remarkable change: its vocal musculature came under operant control. Like other species, it had up to that point displayed warning cries, threatening shouts, and other innate responses, but vocal operant behavior made a great difference because it extended the scope of the social environment. Language was born, and with it many important characteristics of human behavior for which a host of mentalistic explanations have been invented.

The very difference between "language" and "verbal behavior" is an example. Language has the character of a thing, something a person acquires and possesses. Psychologists speak of the "acquisition of language" in the child. The words and sentences of which a language is composed are said to be tools used to express meanings, thoughts, ideas, propositions, emotions, needs, desires, and many other things in or on the speaker's mind. A much more productive view is that verbal behavior is behavior. It has a special character only because it is reinforced by its effects on people—at first other people, but eventually the speaker himself. As a result, it is free of the spatial, temporal, and mechanical relations which prevail between operant behavior and nonsocial consequences. If the opening of a door will be reinforcing, a person may grasp the knob, turn it, and push or pull in a given way, but if, instead, he says, "Please open the door," and a listener responds appropriately, the same reinforcing consequence follows. The contingencies are different, and they generate many important differences in the behavior which have long been obscured by mentalistic explanations.

How a person speaks depends upon the practices of the verbal community of which he is a member. A verbal repertoire may be rudimentary or it may display an elaborate topography under many subtle kinds of stimulus control. The contingencies which shape it may be indulgent (as when parents respond to their children's crude approximations to standard forms) or demanding (as in the teaching of diction). Different verbal communities shape and maintain different languages in the same speaker, who then possesses different repertoires having similar effects upon different listeners. Verbal responses are classified as requests, commands, permissions, and so on, depending upon the reasons why the listener responds, the reasons often being attributed to the speaker's intentions or moods. The fact that the energy of a response is not proportional to the magnitude of the result has contributed to the belief in verbal magic (the magician's "Presto chango" converts a handkerchief into a rabbit). Strong responses appear in the absence of an appropriate audience, as Richard III demonstrated when he cried, "A horse! a horse! my kingdom for a horse!" although there was no one to hear him.

Apart from an occasional relevant audience, verbal behavior requires no environmental support. One needs a bicycle to ride a bicycle but not to say "bicycle." As a result, verbal behavior can occur on almost any occasion. An important consequence is that most people find it easier to say "bicycle" silently than to "ride a bicycle silently." Another important consequence is that the speaker also becomes a listener and may richly reinforce his own behavior.

MEANING AND REFERENCE

The term "meaning," though closely associated with verbal behavior, has been used to make some of the distinctions already discussed. Those who have confused behaviorism with structuralism, in its emphasis on form or topography, have complained that it ignores meaning. What is important, they contend, is not what a person is doing but what his behavior means to him; his behavior has a deeper property not unrelated to the purpose, intention, or expectation discussed in Chapter 4. But the meaning of a response is not in its topography or form (that is the mistake of the structuralist, not the behaviorist); it is to be found in its antecedent history. The behaviorist is also accused of describing the environmental setting in physical terms and overlooking what it means to the responding person, but here again the meaning is not in the current setting but in a history of exposure to contingencies in which similar settings have played a part.

In other words, meaning is not properly regarded as a property either of a response or a situation but rather of the contingencies responsible for both the topography of behavior and the control exerted by stimuli. To take a primitive example, if one rat presses a lever to obtain food when hungry while another does so to obtain water when thirsty, the topographies of their behaviors may be indistinguishable, but they may be said to differ in meaning: to one rat pressing the lever "means" food; to the other it "means" water. But these are aspects of the contingencies which have brought behavior under the control of the current occasion.

Similarly, if a rat is reinforced with food when it presses the lever in the presence of a flashing light but with water when the light is steady, then it could be said that the flashing light means food and the steady light means water, but again these are references not to some property of the light but to the contingencies of which the lights have been parts.

The same point may be made, but with many more implications, in speaking of the meaning of verbal behavior. The over-all function of the behavior is crucial. In an archetypal pattern a speaker is in contact with a situation to which a listener is disposed to respond but with which he is not in contact. A verbal response on the part of the speaker makes it possible for the listener to respond appropriately. For example, let us suppose that a person has an appointment, which he will keep by consulting a clock or a watch. If none is available, he may ask someone to tell him the time, and the response permits him to respond effectively. The speaker sees the clock and announces the time; the listener hears the announcement and keeps his appointment. The three terms which appear in the contingencies of reinforcement generating an operant are divided between two people: the speaker responds to the setting, and the listener engages in the behavior and is affected by the consequences. This will happen only if the behaviors of speaker and listener are supported by additional contingencies arranged by the verbal community.

The listener's belief in what the speaker says is like the belief which underlies the probability of any response ("I believe this will work") or the control exerted by any stimulus ("I believe this is the right place"). It depends on past contingencies, and nothing is gained by internalizing them. To define interpersonal trust as "an expectancy held by an individual or a group that the word, promise, verbal or written statement of another individual or group can be relied on" is to complicate matters unnecessarily.

The *meaning of a response for the speaker* includes the

stimulus which controls it (in the example above, the setting on the face of a clock or watch) and possibly aversive aspects of the question, from which a response brings release. The *meaning for the listener* is close to the meaning the clock face would have if it were visible to him, but it also includes the contingencies involving the appointment, which make a response to the clock face or the verbal response probable at such a time. A person who will leave for an appointment upon seeing a certain position of the hands of a clock will also leave upon hearing a response made by a person whose responses in the past have been accurately controlled by the position of the hands and which for that reason control strong responses now.

One of the unfortunate implications of communication theory is that the meanings for speaker and listener are the same, that something is made common to both of them, that the speaker conveys an idea or meaning, transmits information, or imparts knowledge, as if his mental possessions then become the mental possessions of the listener. There are no meanings which are the same in the speaker and listener. Meanings are not independent entities. We may look for the meaning of a word in the dictionary, but dictionaries do not give meanings; at best they give other words having the same meanings. We must come to a dictionary already "provided with meanings."

A referent might be defined as that aspect of the environment which exerts control over the response of which it is said to be the referent. It does so because of the reinforcing practices of a verbal community. In traditional terms, meanings and referents are not to be found in words but in the circumstances under which words are used by speakers and understood by listeners, but "used" and "understanding" need further analysis.

Verbal responses are often said to be taken by the listener as signs, or symbols, of the situations they describe, and a great deal has been made of the symbolic process, some examples of which we shall consider in the following chapter. Certain atmospheric conditions may be a "sign of rain," and we respond to them to avoid getting wet. We usually respond in a slightly different way in escaping from the rain itself if we have had no sign of it in advance. We can say the same thing about the weatherman's verbal responses, which are no more a sign or symbol of rain than the atmospheric change.

Metaphor.   We have seen that a stimulus present when a response is reinforced acquires some control over the probability that that response will occur, and that this effect generalizes: stimuli sharing some of its properties also acquire some control. In verbal behavior one kind of response evoked by a merely similar stimulus is called a metaphor. The response is not transferred from one situation to another, as the etymology might suggest; it simply occurs because of a similarity in stimuli. Having come to say "explode" in connection with firecrackers or bombs, a person may describe a friend who suddenly behaves in a violent manner as "exploding in anger." Other figures of speech illustrate other behavioral processes.

Abstraction.   A characteristic feature of verbal behavior, directly attributable to special contingencies of reinforcement, is abstraction. It is the listener, not the speaker, who takes practical action with respect to the stimuli controlling a verbal response, and as a result the behavior of the speaker may come under the control of properties of a stimulus to which no practical response is appropriate. A person learns to react to red things under the nonsocial contingencies of his environment, but he does so only by emitting a practical response for each red thing. The contingencies cannot bring a single response under the control of the property of redness alone. But a single property may be important to the listener who takes many kinds of practical action on many different occasions because of it and who therefore reinforces appropriately when a given object is called red. The referent for red can never be identified in any one setting. If we show a person a red pencil and say, "What is that?" and he says, "Red," we cannot tell what property evoked his response, but if we show him many red objects and he always says, "Red," we can do so—and with increasing accuracy as we multiply cases. The speaker is always responding to a physical object, not to "redness" as an abstract entity, and he responds "red" not because he possesses a concept of redness but because special contingencies have brought that response under the control of that property of stimuli.

There is no point in asking how a person can "know the abstract entity called redness." The contingencies explain the behavior, and we need not be disturbed because it is impossible to discover the referent in any single instance. We need not, with William of Ockham and the Nominalists, deny that abstract entities exist and insist that such responses are merely words. What exist are the contingencies which bring behavior under the control of properties or of classes of objects defined by properties. (We can determine that a single response is under the control of one property by naming it. For example, if we show a person a pencil and say, "What *color* is this?" he wil then respond to the property specified as color—provided he has been subject to an appropriate history of reinforcement.)

Concepts.   When a class is defined by more than one property, the referent is usually called a concept rather than an abstract entity. That concepts have real referents has been pointed out by saying that "they are discoveries rather than inventions—they represent reality." In other words, they exist in the world before anyone identifies them. But discovery (as well as invention) suggests mental action in the production of a concept. A concept is simply a feature of a set of contingencies which exist in the world, and it is discovered simply in the sense that the contingencies bring behavior under its control. The statement "Scientific concepts enable certain aspects of the enormous complexity of the world to be handled by men's minds" is vastly improved by substituting "human beings" for "men's minds."

SENTENCES AND PROPOSITIONS

The traditional notion of meaning and referent runs into trouble when we begin to analyze larger verbal responses under the control of more complex environmental circumstances. What are the referents of sentences—not to mention paragraphs, chapters, or books? A sentence surely means more than its separate words mean. Sentences do more than refer to things; they *say* things. But what are the things they say? A traditional answer is "Propositions." But propositions are as elusive as meanings. Bertrand Russell's view has been paraphrased as follows: "The significance of a sentence is that which is common to a sentence in one language and its translation into another language. For example, 'I am hungry' and 'J'ai faim' have in common elements which constitute the significance of a sentence. This common element is the proposition." But what *is* this common element? Where is it to be found? A dictionary that gave the meanings of sentences would simply contain other sentences having the same meanings.

A translation can best be defined as a verbal stimulus that has the same effect as the original (or as much of the same effect as possible) on a different verbal community. A French translation of an English book is not another statement of a set of propositions; it is another sample of verbal behavior having an effect upon a French reader similar to the effect of the English version on an English reader. The same interpretation may be made of a translation from one medium into another. It has been said that the Prelude to *Tristan and Isolde* is "an astonishingly intense and faithful translation into music of the emotions which accompany the union of a pair of lovers." Rather than try to identify the feeling, let alone the proposition, which is thus translated, we may say simply that the music has something of the same effect as physical union.

The concepts of expression and communication may be treated in a similar way. A speaker or a listener responds to conditions of his body which he has learned to call feelings, but what he says or hears is behavior, due to contingencies of which the felt conditions may be by-products. To say that music expresses "what is inexpressible in cognitive, and especially in scientific, language" is to say that it has an effect that verbal behavior cannot have. Verbal behavior does not communicate feelings, though it may result in conditions similarly felt. It does not communicate propositions or instructions. To "instruct" a mother cat to desert her young by delivering an electric shock to a part of her brain does not communicate an instruction that was first held in the mind of the scientist; the shock simply has an effect (a dash of cold water would have produced the same result). Von Frisch's account of the language of bees (an account which is becoming increasingly suspect) did not make him a Champollion, reading a Rosetta stone.

The concept of stimulus control replaces the notion of referent with respect not only to responses which occur in isolation and are called words (such as nouns and adjectives) but also to those complex responses called sentences. Possibly could be said to describe "fact" a referrent of the latter, although its suggestion of truth versus falsity raises difficulties. The child responds in sentences to events in his environment—events involving more than one property or thing, or relations among things, or relations of actor and acted upon, and so on, and his responses contain elements which he never has any occasion to emit alone. The linguist assigns these elements to syntax or grammar. He does so as part of an analysis of the practices of a given verbal community, from which he extracts rules which may be used in the construction of new sentences, as we shall see in Chapter 8.

THE MANIPULATION OF WORDS AND SENTENCES

Structuralism has been strongly encouraged in linguistics because verbal behavior often seems to have an independent status. We are inclined to give special attention to its form because we can report it easily, and rather accurately, simply by modeling it, as in a direct quotation. The report "He said, 'hammer' " gives a much more complete description of the topography of his behavior than "He was hammering." In teaching a child to talk, or an adult to pronounce a difficult word, we produce a model—that is, we say the word and arrange contingencies under which a response having similar properties will be reinforced. There is nothing especially verbal about modeling (in teaching sports or the dance, the instructor "shows a person what to do" in the sense of doing it himself), but with the invention of the alphabet, it became possible to record verbal behavior, and the records, free of any supporting environment, seemed to have an independent existence. A speaker is said to "know" a poem or an oath or a prayer. Early education in China and Greece was largely a matter of memorizing literary works. The student seemed to know the wisdom expressed by the work, even though his behavior was not necessarily under the control of the conditions which induced the original speaker or writer, or an informed listener, to respond in a given way.

Verbal behavior has this kind of independent status when it is in transmission between speaker and listener—for example, when it is the "information" passing over a telephone wire or between writer and reader in the form of a text. Until fairly recently, linguistics and literary criticism confined themselves almost exclusively to the analyses of written records. If these had any meaning, it was the meaning for the reader, since the circumstances under which the behavior had been produced by the writer had been forgotten, if they were ever known.

The availability of verbal behavior in this apparently objective form has caused a great deal of trouble. By dividing such records into words and sentences without regard to the conditions under which the behavior was emitted, we neglect the meaning for the speaker or writer, and almost half the field of verbal behavior therefore escapes attention. Worse still, bits of recorded speech are moved about to compose new "sentences," which are then analyzed for their truth or falsity (in terms of their effect on a reader or listener), although they were never generated by a speaker. Both logician and linguist tend to create new sentences in this way, which they then treat as if they were the records of emitted verbal behavior. If we take the sentence "The sun is a star" and put the word "not" in the proper place, we transform it into "The sun is not a star" but no one has emitted this instance of a verbal response, and it does not describe a fact or express a proposition. It is simply the result of a mechanical process.

Perhaps there is no harm in playing with sentences in this way or in analyzing the kinds of transformations which do or do not make sentences acceptable to the ordinary reader, but it is still a waste of time, particularly when the sentences thus generated could not have been emitted as verbal behavior. A classical example is a paradox, such as "This sentence is false," which appears to be true if false and false if true. The important thing to consider is that no one could ever have emitted the sentence as verbal behavior. A sentence must be in existence before a speaker can say, "This sentence is false," and the response itself will not serve, since it did not exist until it was emitted. What the logician or linguist calls a sentence is not necessarily verbal behavior in any sense which calls for a behavioral analysis.

The transformational rules which generate sentences acceptable to a listener may be of interest, but even so it is a mistake to suppose that verbal behavior is generated by them. Thus, we may analyze the behavior of small children and discover that, for example, part of their speech consists of a small class of "modifiers" and a larger class of "nouns." (This fact about verbal behavior is due to the contingencies of reinforcement arranged by most verbal communities.) It does not follow that the child "forms a noun phrase of a given type" by "selecting first one word from the small class of modifiers and selecting second one word from the large class of nouns." This is a linguist's reconstruction after the fact.

The analysis of verbal behavior, particularly the so-called discovery of grammar, came very late. For thousands of years no one could have known he was speaking according to rule. What happens when rules are discovered will be considered in Chapter 8.

Development.   An undue concern for the structure of verbal behavior has encouraged the metaphor of development or growth. Length of utterance is plotted as a function of age, and semantic and grammatical features are observed as they "develop." The growth of language in a child is easily compared with the growth of an embryo, and grammar can then be attributed to rules possessed by the child at birth. A program in the form of a genetic code is said to "initiate and guide early learning . . . as a child acquires language." But the human species did not evolve because of an inbuilt design: it evolved through selection under contingencies of survival, as the child's verbal behavior evolves under the selective action of contingencies of reinforcement. As I have noted, the world of a child develops, too.

A child does seem to acquire a verbal repertoire at an amazing speed, but we should not overestimate the accomplishment or attribute it to invented linguistic capacities. A child may "learn to use a new word" as the effect of a single reinforcement, but it learns to do nonverbal things with comparable speed. The verbal behavior is impressive in part because the topography is conspicuous and easily identified and in part because it suggests hidden meanings.

If the structuralists and developmentalists had not confined themselves so narrowly to the topography of behavior at the expense of the other parts of the contingencies of reinforcement, we should know much more about how a child learns to speak. We know the words a child first uses and the characteristic orders in which they tend to be used. We know the length of utterances at given ages, and so on. If structure were enough, that would be the whole story. But a record of topography needs to be supplemented by an equally detailed record of the conditions under which it was acquired. What speech has the child heard? Under what circumstances has he heard it? What effects has he achieved when he has uttered similar responses? Until we have this kind of information, the success or failure of any analysis of verbal behavior cannot be judged.

CREATIVE VERBAL BEHAVIOR

In verbal behavior, as in all operant behavior, original forms of response are evoked by situations to which a person has not previously been exposed. The origin of behavior is not unlike the origin of species. New combinations of stimuli appear in new settings, and responses which describe them may never have been made by the speaker before, or heard or read by him in the speech of others. There are many behavioral processes generating "mutations," which are then subject to the selective action of contingencies of reinforcement. We all produce novel forms—for example, in neologisms, blends, portmanteau words, witty remarks involving distortion, and the mistakes of hasty speech.

A great deal has been made of the fact that a child will "invent" a weak past tense for a strong verb, as in saying "he goed" instead of "he went." If he has never heard the form "goed" (that is, if he has associated only with adults), he must have created a new form. But we do not speak of "creation" if, having acquired a list of color words and a list of object words, he for the first time says "purple automobile." The fact that the terminal "-ed" suggests "grammar" is unnecessarily exciting. It is quite possible that it is a separable operant, as a separate indicator of the past tense or of completed action in another language might be, and that "go" and a terminal "-ed" are put together, as "purple" and "automobile" are put together, on a novel occasion. The so-called creative aspect of verbal behavior will be mentioned again later.

7
Thinking

In mentalistic formulations the physical environment is moved into the mind and becomes experience. Behavior is moved into the mind as purpose, intention, ideas, and acts of will. Perceiving the world and profiting from experience become "general-purpose cognitive activities," and abstract and conceptual thinking has sometimes been said to have no external reference at all. Given such well-established precedents, it is not surprising that certain remaining behavioral functions should also be moved inside. Total internalization was recently announced by three cognitive psychologists who, upon completing a book, are said to have declared themselves "subjective behaviorists."

In this chapter I consider a number of behavioral processes which have given rise to the invention of what are usually called higher mental processes. They compose one great part of the field of thinking. It is a difficult field, and no one, so far as I know, claims to give a definitive account. The present analysis is short of perfection for another reason: it must be brief. But if a behavioristic interpretation of thinking is not all we should like to have, it must be remembered that mental or cognitive explanations are not explanations at all.

"Thinking" often means "behaving weakly," where the weakness may be due, for example, to defective stimulus control. Shown an object with which we are not very familiar, we may say, "I think it is a kind of wrench," where "I think" is clearly opposed to "I know." We report a low probability for a different reason when we say, "I think I shall go," rather than "I shall go" or "I know I shall go."

There are more important uses of the term. Watching a chess game, we may wonder "what a player is thinking of" when he makes a move. We may mean that we wonder what he will do next. In other words, we wonder about his incipient or inchoate behavior. To say, "He was thinking of moving his rook," is perhaps to say, "He was on the point of moving it." Usually, however, the term refers to completed behavior which occurs on a scale so small that it cannot be detected by others. Such behavior is called covert. The commonest examples are verbal, because verbal behavior requires no environmental support and because, as both speaker and listener, a person can talk to himself effectively; but nonverbal behavior may also be covert. Thus, what a chess player has in mind may be other moves he has made as he has played the game covertly to test the consequences.

Covert behavior has the advantage that we can act without committing ourselves; we can revoke the behavior and try again if private consequences are not reinforcing. (It is usually only when behavior has been emitted, by the way, that one speaks of an act of will; the term suggests taking a stand and accepting the irrevocable consequences.) Covert behavior is almost always acquired in overt form, and no one has ever shown that the covert form achieves anything which is out of reach of the overt. Covert behavior is also easily observed and by no means unimportant, and it was a mistake for methodological behaviorism and certain versions of logical positivism and structuralism to neglect it simply because it was not "objective." It would also be a mistake not to recognize its limitations. It is far from an adequate substitute for traditional views of thinking. It does not explain overt behavior: it is simply more behavior to be explained.

The present argument is this: mental life and the world in which it is lived are inventions. They have been invented on the analogy of external behavior occurring under external contingencies. Thinking is behaving. The mistake is in allocating the behavior to the mind. Several examples showing how this has been done may be considered.

THE "COGNITIVE" CONTROL OF STIMULI

The ancient view that perception is a kind of capturing or taking possession of the world is encouraged by the real distinction we make between seeing and looking at, hearing and listening to, smelling and sniffing, tasting and savoring, and feeling and feeling of, where the second term in each pair does indeed refer to an act. It is an act which makes a stimulus more effective. By sniffing, for example, we throw air against the surfaces containing the sense organs of smell, and as a result we can detect an odor we might otherwise miss. We also act to reduce stimulation; we squint or shut our eyes, plug our ears, spit, hold our breath, or pull our hand away from a painful object. Some of these "precurrent," or preparatory, behaviors are part of our genetic endowment; others are produced by contingencies of reinforcement.

A rather similar process can be demonstrated as follows: A hungry pigeon is occasionally reinforced with food when it pecks a circular disk on the wall of an experimental chamber. If it is reinforced when the disk is red but not when it is green, it eventually stops pecking when the disk is green. Unfortunately for the pigeon, the color washes out and becomes difficult or impossible to detect. The pigeon can strengthen the color by pecking another disk, however, and it will do so as long as the color remains important. The production of additional stimuli favoring a discriminative response is a familiar part of science. In testing the acidity of a solution, for example, another solution is added, and if the color changes in a specified way, the acidity can be determined.

Analogous mental or cognitive activities have been invented. We attend to a stimulus or ignore it without changing any physical condition (for example, we can listen to a particular instrument in recorded music, in part by suppressing our responses to the other instruments), and we are said to do so with various mental mechanisms. Radio and television are presumably responsible for the current metaphor of "tuning the world in or out." An older metaphor, resembling Maxwell's Demon in the second law of thermodynamics, portrays a kind of gatekeeper—a loyal servant who admits wanted stimuli and defends his master against unwanted. It has been said to be "conceivable that the nervous system actually switches off one ear in order to listen to the other." We have not explained anything, of course, until we have explained the behavior of the gatekeeper, and any effort to do so will suffice to explain the change in stimulus control.

What is involved in attention is not a change of stimulus or of receptors but the contingencies underlying the process of discrimination. We pay attention or fail to pay attention to a lecturer or a traffic sign depending upon what has happened in the past under similar circumstances. Discrimination is a behavioral process: the contingencies, not the mind, make discriminations. We say that a person discerns or "makes out" an object in a fog or at a great distance in the sense that he eventually responds to it correctly. Discern, like discriminate, may mean an act favoring a response (it may be closer to "look at" than to "see"), but it need not be. We discern the important things in a given setting because of past contingencies in which they have been important.

Abstracting and forming concepts are likely to be called cognitive, but they also involve contingencies of reinforcement. We do not need to suppose that an abstract entity or concept is held in the mind; a subtle and complex history of reinforcement has generated a special kind of stimulus control. It is commonly said that concepts "unify our thoughts," but the evidence seems to be that they simply enable us to talk about features of the world common to a large assortment of instances. One scientist has said that "there is excellent reason to believe that the whole of chemistry is explicable in terms of electrons and the wave functions which describe their location. This is an enormous simplification of thought." It is certainly an enormous simplification—or would be, if feasible—but it is the simplification of verbal and practical behavior rather than of thought. The same writer has said that concepts are "discoveries as well as—indeed, more than—inventions" and that they are "an exercise of the human mind which represents reality," but he confesses that the nature of the relationship is a mystery. It is the mystery of the abstract entity rather than of the available facts. The referents of concepts are in the real world; they are not ideas in the mind of the scientist. They are discoveries or inventions simply in the sense that a verbal environment has evolved in which obscure properties of nature are brought into the control of human behavior. It is probably too late to trace the emergence of concepts such as mass, energy, or temperature, even with the help of the historian of science, and their current use is perhaps as difficult to analyze; but nothing is gained by putting them in the mind of the scientist.

An example from a popular article on place learning shows how troublesome it is to explain behavior by inventing a concept instead of by pursuing contingencies. Children who have been taught to complete the expressions "3 + 6" by saying "9" are then shown "6 + 3." "One child is hopelessly puzzled, another readily answers 9. It is clear that the two pupils have learned different things: the first child has learned a specific answer to a specific question; the second has learned an arithmetical concept." But what does this tell us? Can we be sure that the second child has not also been taught to say "9" to "6 + 3" at some other time? Has he perhaps learned a large number of instances such as "1 + 2 = 2 + 1" and "1 + 3 = 3 + 1"? Has he learned to state the rule of commutation and to exemplify it? If we are content to speak of an arithmetical concept, we shall never find out what the child has actually learned.

SEARCH AND RECALL

Another so-called cognitive activity which affects a person's contact with controlling stimuli is search. To look for something is to behave in ways which have been reinforced when something has turned up. We say that a hungry animal moves about looking for food. The fact that it is active, and even the fact that it is active in particular ways, may be part of its genetic endowment, explained in turn by the survival value of the behavior, but the way in which an organism looks for food in a familiar environment is clearly dependent upon its past successes. We tell a child to find his shoe, and the child starts to look in places where shoes have been found.

There are, however, more specialized strategies of looking for things. What does one do to find an object in a box of rubbish ("scrutinize" comes from an expression having to do with the sorting out of trash) or on the shelves of a warehouse? How does one go about finding a word on a page or finding and crossing out all the *a*'s in a column of print? The skillful searcher moves about, sorts out materials, and moves his eyes in ways which maximize the chances of finding things and minimize the chances of missing, and he does so because of past contingencies. We have no reason to call the behavior cognitive, but a rather similar process is said to take place in the world of the mind.

For various reasons, suggested by such terms as "memorandum," "memento," "souvenir," and "memorial," people have made copies of the world around them, as well as records about what has happened in that world, and have stored them for future use. Familiar examples are scratches on clay tablets, engraved legends on monuments, books, paintings, photographs, phonographic recordings, and the magnetic stores of computers. On a future occasion such a record can evoke behavior appropriate to an earlier occasion and may permit a person to respond more effectively. The practice has led to the elaboration of a cognitive metaphor, no doubt antedating by centuries any psychological system-making, in which experiences are said to be stored in memory, later to be retrieved or recalled and used in order to behave more effectively in a current setting.

What is said to be stored are copies of stimuli—faces, names, dates, texts, places, and so on—which when retrieved have some of the effect of the originals. The copies cannot have the dimensions of the originals; they must be transduced and encoded—possibly as engrams, reverberating circuits, or electrical fields. Storage is particularly hard to imagine for the memory of a musical composition or a story, which has temporal properties. Nevertheless, all these things are said to "reside" in memory.

But what is the mental parallel of physical search? How are we to go about finding an item in the storehouse of memory? Plato raised a fundamental question: "A man cannot inquire either about that which he knows or about that which he does not know; for if he knows he has no need to inquire; and if not, he cannot, for he does not know the very subject about which he is to inquire." For "inquire" read "search." If we can remember a name, we have no need to search our memory; if we cannot remember it, how do we go about looking for it? The cognitive psychologist talks about various systems of access borrowed from the filing systems of libraries, computers, warehouses, postal systems, and so on. Thus, the superior retrieval of certain kinds of items is attributed to "an addressing system that allows immediate access to items"—as it certainly should!

In a behavioral analysis probability is substituted for accessibility. The contingencies which affect an organism are not stored by it. They are never inside it; they simply change it. As a result, the organism behaves in special ways under special kinds of stimulus control. Future stimuli are effective if they resemble the stimuli which have been part of earlier contingencies; an incidental stimulus may "remind" us of a person, place, or event if it has some resemblance to that person, place, or event. Being reminded means being made likely to respond, possibly perceptually. A name may remind us of a person in the sense that we now see him. This does not mean conjuring up a copy of the person which we then look at; it simply means behaving as we behaved in his presence upon some earlier occasion. There was no copy of his visual appearance inside us then, as there is none now. The incidental stimulus does not send us off in search of a stored copy, which we perceive anew when we find it.

The extensive experiments by cognitive psychologists on accessibility can all be reinterpreted in terms of probability. If familiar words are more quickly recalled than strange ones, it is because they have a greater initial probability, due to the history alluded to by the word "familiar." We do not need to conclude that "the word store has a form of organization which allows quicker access to the more commonly required items than to the rarer ones."

Techniques of recall are not concerned with searching a storehouse of memory but with increasing the probability of responses. Mnemonics are pre-learned or easily learned behaviors which prompt or otherwise strengthen the behavior to be recalled. If we have forgotten the next part of a piece of music we are playing or a poem we are reciting, we go back for a running start, not because the music or poem has been stored as a unit of memory, so that one part helps us find the other part, but because the extra stimulation we generate in the running start is sufficient to evoke the forgotten passage. In recalling a name it is useful to go through the alphabet, not because we have stored all the names we know in alphabetical order but because pronouncing the sound of a letter is pronouncing part of the name; we prompt the response in ourselves as we prompt it in someone else whom we are helping to recall it. When, in recalling a name, we find a wrong name too powerful, it is not because the wrong name "masks the target" in our storehouse of memory but because it is repeatedly emitted to the exclusion of the name we are recalling. Techniques of learning to observe in such a way that one remembers more readily are not techniques of storage but rather of generating effective perception. The artist looking at a scene which he will later sketch will to some extent sketch it as he looks, thus strengthening the kind of behavior which will be important to him later.

The metaphor of storage in memory, which has seemed to be so dramatically confirmed by the computer, has caused a great deal of trouble. The computer is a bad model—as bad as the clay tablets on which the metaphor was probably first based. We do make external records for future use, to supplement defective contingencies of reinforcement, but the assumption of a parallel inner record-keeping process adds nothing to our understanding of this kind of thinking. (It is not the behaviorist, incidentally, but the cognitive psychologist, with his computer-model of the mind, who represents man as a machine.)

SOLVING PROBLEMS

Other so-called cognitive processes have to do with solving problems. It is a field marked by a great deal of mystery, part of it due to the way in which it has been formulated. Problems need to be solved, we are told, because a person needs "to orient himself in an infinitely complex reality, to order the endless particularity of experience, to find essences behind facts, to attach meaning to being-in-the-world." Fortunately, a much simpler statement is possible. A person has a problem when some condition will be reinforcing but he lacks a response that will produce it. He will solve the problem when he emits such a response. For example, introducing someone whose name one has forgotten is a problem which is solved by recalling or otherwise learning the name. An algebraic equation is solved by finding the value of x. The problem of a stalled car is solved by starting the car. The problem of an illness is solved by finding an effective treatment. Solving a problem is, however, more than *emitting* the response which is the solution; it is a matter of taking steps to make that response more probable, usually by changing the environment. Thus, if the problem is to say whether two things are the same or different, we may put them side by side to facilitate a comparison; if it is to make sure that we shall treat them as different, we separate them. We group similar things in classes in order to treat them in the same way. We put things in order if the solution requires a series of steps. We restate a verbal response by translating it from words into symbols. We represent the premises of a syllogism with overlapping circles. We clarify quantities by counting and measuring. We confirm a solution by solving a problem a second time, possibly in a different way.

We learn some of these strategies from the problematic contingencies to which we are exposed, but not much can be learned in a single lifetime, and an important function of a culture is to transmit what others have learned. Whether problem solving arises from raw contingencies or from instruction by others, it is acquired in overt form (with the possible exception of a strategy learned at the covert level from private consequences) and can always be carried out at the overt level. The covert case, to which the term "thinking" is most likely to be applied, enjoys no special advantage beyond that of speed or confidentiality.

Choice.   A problem to which a good deal of attention has been given arises when two or more responses appear to be possible and a person chooses or decides among them. The problem is to escape from indecision rather than to discover an effective response. We facilitate choosing or making a decision in various ways—for example, by "reviewing the facts." If we are working with external materials, verbal or otherwise, we may indeed re-view them in the sense of looking at them again. If, however, we are working covertly, we do not recover the facts, as if we were pulling papers out of a file; we merely see them again. In reviewing an argument we simply argue again. Re-viewing is not re-calling, since all the facts to be used are available.

It is said that a person has made a choice when he has taken one of two or more seemingly possible courses of action. The trouble lies in the word possible. Simply to make one of several "possible" responses—as in walking aimlessly through a park—requires no serious act of decision, but when consequences are important and the probabilities of two or more responses are nearly equal, a problem must be solved. A person usually solves it and escapes from indecision by changing the setting.

To say that "humans can make choices and desire to do so" simply means that a situation in which two or more responses are about equally probable may be aversive, and that any decision-making behavior which strengthens one response and makes the other unlikely is reinforced. To say that "humans require freedom to exercise the choices they are capable of making" adds further complications. To exercise a choice is simply to act, and the choice a person is capable of making is the act itself. The person requires freedom to make it simply in the sense that he can make it only if there are no restraints, either in the physical situation or in other conditions affecting his behavior.

It is easy to overlook the behavior which actually solves a problem. In one classical account, a chimpanzee seemed to have fitted two sticks together in order to rake in a banana which was otherwise out of reach through the bars of his cage. To say that the chimpanzee showed "intelligent behavior based on a perception of what was required to solve the problem: some way of overcoming the distance barrier" is to make it almost impossible to discover what happened. To solve such a problem a chimpanzee must have learned at least the following: to stop reaching for a banana out of reach; to stop reaching with short sticks; to discriminate between long and short sticks, as by using long sticks to rake in bananas successfully; to pick up two sticks in separate hands; and to thrust sticks into holes. With this preparation, it is not impossible that in that rare (but poorly authenticated) instance the chimpanzee stuck one stick into the hole at the end of another and used the resulting long stick to rake in the banana.

The importance of the behavioral analysis is clear whenever we undertake to do anything about problem solving. To teach comparable behavior to a child, for example, we should at some time or other have to emphasize all these ingredients. It is doubtful whether we could make much progress by impressing the child with "the need to overcome a distance barrier."

CREATIVE BEHAVIOR

The creative mind has never been without its problems, as the classical discussion in Plato's *Meno* suggests. It was an insoluble problem for stimulus-response psychology because if behavior were nothing but responses to stimuli, the stimuli might be novel but not the behavior. Operant conditioning solves the problem more or less as natural selection solved a similar problem in evolutionary theory. As accidental traits, arising from mutations, are selected by their contribution to survival, so accidental variations in behavior are selected by their reinforcing consequences.

That chance can play a part in the production of anything as important as mathematics, science, or art has often been questioned. Moreover, at first glance, there seems to be no room for chance in any completely determined system. The Church, in its belief in a predestined master plan, censured Montaigne for using words like fortune and nature, and if Saint Augustine sought heavenly counsel by opening his Bible and reading the first words that met his eyes, it was only because they did not meet his eyes by chance. Another deterministic system, psychoanalysis, has initiated another age in which chance is taboo; for the strict Freudian, no one can forget an appointment or call a person by the wrong name or make a slip of the tongue by chance. Yet the biographies of writers, composers, artists, scientists, mathematicians, and inventors all reveal the importance of happy accidents in the production of original behavior.

The concept of selection is again the key. The mutations in genetic and evolutionary theory are random, and the topographies of response selected by reinforcement are, if not random, at least not necessarily related to the contingencies under which they will be selected. And creative thinking is largely concerned with the production of "mutations." Explicit ways of making it more likely that original behavior will occur by introducing "mutations" are familiar to writers, artists, composers, mathematicians, scientists, and inventors. Either the setting or the topography of behavior may be deliberately varied. The painter varies his colors, brushes, and surfaces to produce new textures and forms. The composer generates new rhythms, scales, melodies, and harmonic sequences, sometimes through the systematic permutation of older forms, possibly with the help of mathematical or mechanical devices. The mathematician explores the results of changing a set of axioms. The results may be reinforcing in the sense that they are beautiful or, in most of mathematics and in science and invention, successful.

Novel verbal responses are likely to be generated by discussion, not only because more than one history of reinforcement is then active but also because different histories may by accident or design lead to novel settings. The so-called history of ideas offers many examples. In the eighteenth century in France the leaders of the Enlightenment borrowed a good deal from English writers—in particular, Bacon, Locke, and Newton. As one author has put it, "English thoughts in French heads produced in the long run some astonishing and explosive consequences." The sentence is intentionally metaphorical, of course, and mixes the mental ("thoughts") with the anatomical ("heads"), but it makes the valid point that translations from English into French that are then read by people with very different verbal histories may generate novel responses.

THE STRUCTURE OF MIND

The structure of thought and the development of the mind have, of course, been popular themes for centuries. As we shall see in the next two chapters, there are certain objective states of knowledge, but thought processes are behavioral, and a structuralist account is necessarily incomplete if it neglects genetic and personal histories. The development of thinking has been most often described with horticultural metaphors. The growth of the mind is a central figure. The teacher is to cultivate the mind as a farmer cultivates his fields, and the intellect is to be trained as a vine is trained in a vineyard. Meanwhile the development of the world to which a thinking person is exposed is overlooked.

We have noted that those who study the "development of language" in the child tell us much about vocabulary, grammar, and length of sentences but very little about the hundreds of thousands of occasions upon which a child hears words and sentences spoken or the many thousands of times he himself speaks them with results, and that no adequate account of the "development of language" is therefore possible. We may say the same thing for the growth of the mind. The behavior which is said to indicate the possession of the concept of inertia and the age at which it normally appears are no doubt important facts, but we should also know something about the many thousands of occasions upon which a child has pushed, pulled, twisted, and turned things in "developing" that concept.

In the absence of any adequate account of the development or growth of a person's exposure to an environment, the almost inevitable result is that important aspects of thinking are assigned to genetic endowment. Not only is verbal behavior said to show the operation of innate rules of grammar, but "innate ideas such as size, shape, motion, position, number, and duration" are said to "give form and meaning to the confused fragmentary data that we experience every day in our lives." Size, shape, motion, position, number, and duration are features of the *environment*. They have prevailed long enough and behavior with respect to them has been crucial enough to make the evolution of appropriate behavior possible, but contingencies of reinforcement are at work every day in the life of the individual to generate supplementary behavior under the control of the same features. The greatest achievements of the human species (not of the human mind) have occurred too recently to make a genetic explanation defensible, but whether we appeal to contingencies of survival or contingencies of reinforcement we can at least dispense with the appeal to in-

THE THINKING MIND

nate ideas. It may be true that there is no structure without construction, but we must look to the constructing environment, not to a constructing mind,

Mind is said to play an important role in thinking. It is sometimes spoken of as the place where thinking occurs, where one image, memory, or idea leads to another in a "stream of consciousness." It can be empty or filled with facts; it can be ordered or chaotic. "Mathematics," says a prestige advertisement of a telephone company, "happens in the mind. . . . It is essentially a thing of the mind, for it works through concepts, symbols, and relationships." Sometimes the mind appears to be the instrument of thinking; it can be keen or dull, muddled by alcohol or cleared by a brisk walk. But usually it is the thinking agent. It is the mind which is said to examine sensory data and make inferences about the outside world, to store and retrieve records, to filter incoming information, to put bits of information in pigeonholes, to make decisions, and to will to act.

In all these roles it has been possible to avoid the problems of dualism by substituting "brain" for "mind." The brain is the place where thinking is said to take place; it is the instrument of thinking and may be keen or dull; and it is the agent which processes incoming data and stores them in the form of data structures. Both the mind and the brain are not far from the ancient notion of a homunculus—an inner person who behaves in precisely the ways necessary to explain the behavior of the outer person in whom he dwells.

A much simpler solution is to identify the mind with the person. Human thought is human behavior. The history of human thought is what people have said and done. Mathematical symbols are the products of written and spoken verbal behavior, and the concepts and relationships of which they are symbols are in the environment. Thinking has the dimensions of behavior, not of a fancied inner process which finds expression in behavior.

We are only just beginning to understand the effects of complex contingencies of reinforcement, but if our analysis of the behavior called thinking is still defective, the facts to be treated are nevertheless relatively clear-cut and accessible. In contrast, the world of the mind is as remote today as it was when Plato is said to have discovered it. By attempting to move human behavior into a world of nonphysical dimensions, mentalistic or cognitive psychologists have cast the basic issues in insoluble forms. They have also probably cost us much useful evidence, because great thinkers (who presumably know what thinking is) have been led to report their activities in subjective terms, focusing on their feelings and what they introspectively observe while thinking, and as a result they have failed to report significant facts about their earlier histories.

Causes and Reasons

Some important kinds of thinking remain to be considered. The behavior discussed in the last chapter is the product of contingencies of reinforcement; it is what happens when, in a given environmental setting, behavior has certain kinds of consequences. The so-called intellectual life of the mind underwent an important change with the advent of verbal behavior. People began to talk about what they were doing and why they were doing it. They described their behavior, the setting in which it occurred, and the consequences. In other words, in addition to being affected by contingencies of reinforcement, they began to analyze them.

COMMANDS, ADVICE, AND WARNINGS

One of the first verbal practices of this sort must have been giving orders or commands. "Move over!" describes an act and implies a consequence: the listener is to move over—or else! The speaker tells the listener what he is to do and arranges aversive consequences under which he learns to do it and to do it again whenever the order is repeated. A warning usually differs from an order or command because the aversive consequences are not arranged by the person who issues it: "Watch out!" describes an act and implies a consequence, such as escape from a falling rock, but the latter is a natural result of the behavior rather than one contrived by the speaker. Advice ("Go West, young man!") specifies behavior and implies positively reinforcing consequences which are also not contrived by the adviser (". . . and you will make your fortune"). A person heeds warnings and takes advice depending upon what has happened in similar circumstances in the past. As in Chapters 5 and 6, the probability that he will respond could be called a measure of his trust or belief in the speaker or in what the speaker says.

DIRECTIONS AND INSTRUCTIONS

One person gives another directions by noting or implying a reinforcing consequence, by describing behavior having that consequence, and especially by describing the controlling environment: "To get to Boston, follow Route 93 to the intersection with Route 495, turn left on Route 90 . . ." Directions for operating a vending machine describe a series of acts to be undertaken in order: "To operate, place coin in slot and pull plunger beneath item wanted." Directions do not impart knowledge or convey information: they describe behavior to be executed and state or imply consequences.

Instructions are designed to make further direction unnecessary. A person learning to drive a car responds to the verbal behavior of the person sitting beside him; he starts, stops, shifts, signals, and so on when told to do so. These verbal stimuli may at first be directions, but they become instruction if verbal help is given only as needed. The driver's behavior is then eventually taken over by the natural, nonverbal contingencies of driving a car. To learn to drive simply through exposure to those contingencies would take a very long time. The would-be driver would have to discover what happens when he moves the shift lever, turns the wheel, presses on the accelerator, applies the brake, and so on, and all with great danger to himself. By following instructions, he avoids exposure to many of these contingencies and eventually behaves as the instructor himself behaves.

The instructor has not "communicated" his knowledge or his experience to the learner. The final uninstructed behavior is shaped and maintained by the natural contingencies of car and highway. The instructor has made it possible for the learner to come under their control speedily and without harm.

Much of education is instruction in verbal behavior. The student is told how to "use words" rather than how to use an accelerator or brake. In neither case is he given knowledge; he is told how to behave. The instruction given by a labeled picture often works very quickly; the viewer knows at once what an object is called and what the label means. A definition is a seemingly more internal form of instruction, but its effect is simply that one verbal response is now used interchangeably with another.

FOLKLORE, MAXIMS, AND PROVERBS

Some forms of instruction can be transmitted from generation to generation because the contingencies they describe are long-lasting. Such a maxim as "To lose a friend, lend him money" describes behavior (lending money) and a consequence (losing a friend). We might translate La Rochefoucauld's "Self-esteem is the greatest of flatterers" in this way: "We are more likely to say good things about ourselves than about others, and what we say is more likely to be a matter of pleasing the listener than of reporting the facts." The craftsman's rules of thumb are part of folklore and may become permanent features of a culture if they make it easier to teach or remember the behavior they describe. Folklore, maxims, and proverbs are often especially effective because many of the advantages of the behavior they strengthen are long deferred and do not function well as reinforcers.

When social contingencies characteristic of a small, slowly changing community are disturbed, formal directions need to be invoked which were once unnecessary. One writer has noted that until a few decades ago "instinct about the rhythm of the mother tongue served instead of principles. Now explicit ones are needed to fill the place of instinct" (where instinct presumably means behavior directly shaped by the verbal community).

GOVERNMENTAL AND RELIGIOUS LAWS

When people began to live together in groups, a social environment arose, and it was marked by certain practices. Those who behaved in ways injurious to others, for example, were punished by those they injured. Standard warnings could be formulated, as the behavior came to be called bad and punished accordingly, even by those who were not injured by a specific instance. The contingencies became more powerful when they were codified in the religious and governmental warnings, directions, and instructions called laws. By obeying the law a person avoids punishment.

Special contingencies are arranged to enforce governmental and religious laws, but uncontrived social contingencies maintained by the group may have the same effect. Where a law codifies pre-existing social sanctions opposed to stealing, for example, a person may begin by obeying the commandment "Thou shalt not steal," but he may eventually refrain from stealing to avoid the disapproval and criticism of his friends. In doing so he comes under the control of the uncodified social sanctions from which the law was originally derived.

THE LAWS OF SCIENCE

Francis Bacon, a lawyer, seems to have been the first to speak of the laws of science. As a well-governed state owed its order to its laws, so it might be possible to discover the laws responsible for the order in the physical world. Scientific laws probably emerged from the lore of craftsmen, and a simple example will illustrate the difference between behavior shaped by natural contingencies and behavior generated by a rule. In the forge of a medieval blacksmith a large bellows provided the forced draft needed for a hot fire. The bellows was most efficient if one opened it fully before closing it and opened it quickly and closed it slowly. The blacksmith learned to operate the bellows in this way because of the reinforcing result of a steady, hot fire. He could have learned to do so without describing his behavior, but a description may have been helpful in operating the bellows properly or in remembering how to do so after an interval. A short verse served this function:

> Up high,
> Down low,
> Up quick,
> Down slow,
>   And that's the way to blow.

The verse was helpful for a different reason when the blacksmith hired an apprentice; he could tell him how to operate the bellows by teaching him the verse as a rule. The apprentice followed the rule, not because the fire was then steadily hot, but because he was paid for doing so. He need never have seen the effect on the fire. His behavior was entirely rule-governed; the blacksmith's was both contingency-shaped and to some extent rule-governed after he had discovered the rule.

Early scientific laws supplemented the natural contingencies of the physical world. A farmer spading the soil or a mason prizing a stone with a pole was controlled by contingencies involving levers: the soil or stone moved most readily if force was applied as far as possible from the fulcrum. Spades and poles were made long for that reason, and some lore, similar to the blacksmith's rule, may have been used to teach new workers how to choose and where to grasp spades or poles. A more formal statement of the law of the lever permitted the principle to be used in situations where contingency-shaped behavior was unlikely or impossible.

Differences in thought processes have been attributed to the apparent differences between the laws of religion or government and the laws of science. The first are said to be "made," the second merely discovered, but the difference is not in the laws but in the contingencies the laws describe. The laws of religions and governments codify contingencies of reinforcement maintained by social environments. The laws of science describe contingencies which prevail in the environment quite apart from any deliberate human action.

By learning the laws of science, a person is able to behave effectively under the contingencies of an extraordinarily complex world. Science carries him beyond personal experience and beyond the defective sampling of nature inevitable in a single lifetime. It also brings him under the control of conditions which could play no part in shaping and maintaining his behavior. He may stop smoking because of a rule derived from a statistical study of the consequences, although the consequences themselves are too deferred to have any reinforcing effect.

CONTINGENCY-SHAPED VERSUS
RULE-GOVERNED BEHAVIOR

Rules can usually be learned more quickly than the behavior shaped by the contingencies they describe. Most people can learn the instruction "Push down on the gearshift lever before moving it into the reverse position" more readily than the actual shifting movement, especially if the lever does not move easily or if, in other cars with which the driver is familiar, it does not need to be pushed down. Rules make it easier to profit from similarities between contingencies: "This gearshift operates like that in a BMW." Rules are particularly valuable when contingencies are complex or unclear or for any other reason not very effective.

A person may use the rules of a language to speak correctly when he has not been adequately exposed to a verbal community. In learning a second language, for example, he can discover appropriate responses in a two-language dictionary and appropriate rules in a grammar. If these aids are adequate, he can presumably speak correctly, but he would be helpless without the dictionary and the grammar, and even if he memorized both of them, he would still not *know* the language in the sense to be discussed in the following chapter.

A person who is following directions, taking advice, heeding warnings, or obeying rules or laws does not behave precisely as one who has been directly exposed to the contingencies, because a description of the contingencies is never complete or exact (it is usually simplified in order to be easily taught or understood) and because the supporting contingencies are seldom fully maintained. The apprentice who operates the bellows simply because he is paid to do so does not operate it as if he were directly affected by the condition of the fire. Driving a car by following instructions differs from the behavior finally shaped by the movement of the car on a highway. Speaking a language with the help of a dictionary and a grammar is not like speaking it through exposure to a verbal community. The feelings associated with the two kinds of behavior are also different, but they do not explain the difference in the behaviors.

The control exerted by directions, advice, rules, and laws is more conspicuous than that exerted by the contingencies themselves, in part because it is less subtle, and the latter has therefore seemed to mean a greater personal contribution and inner worth. Doing good because one is reinforced by the good of others is more highly honored than doing good because the law demands it. In the first case, the person feels well disposed; in the second, he may feel little more than a fear of punishment. Civic virtue and piety are reserved for those who are not merely following rules. This is necessarily the case when the contingencies have never been analyzed—when, as in poetry or mysticism, they are said to be ineffable.

Rule-following behavior is said to be the veneer of civilization, whereas behavior shaped by natural contingencies comes from the depths of the personality or mind. Artists, composers, and poets sometimes follow rules (imitating the work of others, for example, is a version of rule following), but greater merit attaches to behavior which is due to a personal exposure to an environment. Unlike those who submit to contingencies arranged to support rules, a "natural" artist, composer, or poet will behave in idiosyncratic ways and will be more likely to feel the bodily conditions, called excitement or joy, associated with "natural" reinforcers.

The planned or well-made work may suffer from the suspicion which attaches to any calculated behavior. The intuitive mathematician seems superior to one who must proceed step by step. We naturally object to the calculating friend who has learned how to make friends and influence people. Possibly that is why contingencies sometimes go unexamined or unreported; a description would destroy some of their effect. There are those who "enjoy music and don't want to know why," and Stendhal, noting in his *Journal* the "loveliest evening" he had ever spent, adds, "I know very well the secret of the pleasure I have enjoyed but I will not write it down in order not to tarnish it."

It is a mistake, as I pointed out in Chapter 5, to say that the world described by science is somehow or other closer to "what is really there," but it is also a mistake to say that the personal experience of artist, composer, or poet is closer to "what is really there." All behavior is determined, directly or indirectly, by consequences, and the behaviors of both scientist and nonscientist are shaped by what is really there but in different ways.

ARE THE RULES IN THE CONTINGENCIES?

I have devoted a good deal of space to rule-governed and contingency-shaped behavior for several reasons. One has to do with the problem of knowledge, which is discussed in the next chapter but about which something should be said here. We do not need to describe contingencies of reinforcement in order to be affected by them. Lower organisms presumably do not do so, nor did the human species before it acquired verbal behavior. A person changed by operant reinforcement has not "learned a probability"; he has learned to respond at a given rate because of a given frequency of reinforcement. We do not need to say that "rules are constructed by the mind in the course of the acquisition of knowledge." The mason uses a lever efficiently without knowing the law, and a child or dog learns to catch a ball without "in some sense extracting the rules governing trajectories."

The so-called rules of grammar have recently been the subject of a good deal of controversy. It is said that there are rules and instructions which govern the use of language and which we obey without being aware of them. Certainly for thousands of years people spoke grammatically without knowing that there were rules of grammar. Grammatical behavior was shaped, then as now, by the reinforcing practices of verbal communities in which some behaviors were more effective than others, and sentences were generated by the joint action of past reinforcements and current settings. But it is the contingencies which "govern the use of language," not rules, whether or not they are extracted.

REASON AND REASONS

Possibly the most admired cognitive or mental process is reason. It is said to be a thing of the mind which distinguishes man from the brutes. It was once thought of as a possession, "an essence of innate ideas, granted anterior to experience, by which the absolute being of things is disclosed to us." But by the eighteenth century, according to Cassirer, reason "is much less a possession than it is a mode of acquisition. Reason is not the area, the treasury of the mind, in which truth, like a minted coin, lies protected. Reason is rather the principle and original force of the mind, which impels to the discovery of truth and to the defining and assuring of it." The reference to an impelling force suggests that we are still a long way from a behavioral definition.

We often speak of the consequences of behavior as *reasons*. We cite them in explaining our own behavior: "The reason I went to the bank was to get some money." The term seems more suitable than cause, especially if we have not fully understood the process of selection, because anything which follows behavior does not seem to be in the right place to be the cause of it. Nevertheless, a reason which lies in the future is no more effective than any other future event. It does not become effective because a person "keeps it in mind" or "thinks of it" or "knows the probability that it will occur," for expressions of this sort merely reflect an effort to find a prior representative of a future consequence.

The consequences described or implied in advice, warnings, instructions, and laws are the *reasons why* a person takes advice, heeds warnings, follows instructions, and obeys laws. People are not born with a readiness to follow advice or heed warnings. Stimuli having the status of advice and warnings must play a part in a long history of conditioning before a person can be induced to behave by being given reasons. To give a student reasons why something is worth learning is to point to possibly reinforcing consequences, but they may be long deferred, and the student's behavior will change as a result of the pointing only if the teacher has been part of effective contingencies in the past. When a therapist points to reasons why his patient's behavior is costing him friends, he can be said to "clarify a relation between behavior and certain aversive consequences," but the patient will change only if the therapist makes remarks effective in other ways— not by "building trust or belief" but by making his behavior a part of contingencies in which the patient has been reinforced. (Neither the teacher nor the therapist is resorting to "cognitive input" in such examples.)

REASONING

I: INDUCTION

Induction has been defined as reasoning from part to whole, from particulars to generals. Possibly we may translate by saying that in analyzing instances we can extract rules which apply to classes of events. We have seen that operant conditioning has been said to indicate such a process; an organism reinforced on one or more occasions is said to "infer or judge that similar consequences will follow upon other occasions." Fortunately operant conditioning is effective even when this does not occur, but something like it may occur when a person analyzes the circumstances in which he is living. Induction is not the process by which behavior is strengthened by reinforcement; it is an analysis of the conditions under which behavior is reinforced. The analysis may lead to descriptions which, as we have just seen, can evoke behavior appropriate to the contingencies without direct exposure to them.

A person may solve a problem by changing the setting in which it appears, and a few problem-solving strategies were noted in the last chapter. A person can acquire them as he acquires any behavior, but usually from an instructional social environment. He may also solve a problem by analyzing it in the present sense, because in doing so he arrives at a rule which, when followed, solves the problem. Reasoning about behavior is a matter of analyzing the reasons for behavior, and reasoning about a problem is a matter of looking at the problematical contingencies rather than merely altering them through established problem-solving procedures. Reasoning in this sense steps in when routine methods of problem solving leave off, but it is not that we then move from noncreative to creative measures. The distinction is between the practical manipulation of a setting and the analysis of that setting. Reasoning tells us why standard problem-solving procedures work, just as a statement of contingencies of reinforcement tells us why a person behaves as he does.

Psychoanalytic writers sometimes confuse rational and irrational with conscious and unconscious. (Irrational, like unreasonable, has unfortunate overtones; irrational behavior is not appropriate to current circumstances; it appears to be emitted for the wrong reasons. But this has little if anything to do with the present distinction.) All behavior, effective or not, is at first nonrational in the sense that the contingencies responsible for it have not been analyzed. All behavior is at first unconscious, but it may become conscious without becoming rational: a person may know what he is doing without knowing why he is doing it.

People do not behave irrationally simply because they are not aware of all the variables at issue. It is a step forward to discover that we carry bad news in part because we are reinforced by the discomfiture of our friends and that we mention the name of a person because there is someone in the room who resembles him, although we have not up to this point "seen" him. We may object when this is pointed out, because we may not want to believe, as one writer has put it, that "there is more to human personality than immediate consciousness tells us there is," but what is left out is not to be found in the "transrational region of the mind." We cannot, of course, analyze contingencies which we do not observe, but we can observe them without analyzing them. To act by taking reasons for action into account and to modify one's behavior in terms of that account is more than being aware of what one is doing.

Several aspects of the life of reason deserve comment.

Folly and Reason. Erasmus in his *In Praise of Folly* pointed out that one cannot begin with reason. The life of reason is no doubt admirable, but there would be nothing to be reasonable about if it were not for the effect of food, sex, and other basic reinforcers—the things Erasmus called folly. "The persistence of human folly in the face of heroic efforts to enlighten it" with reason may be the tragedy of our times, but if we are to take effective action, reason will consist of an analysis of the contingencies represented by folly and of the uses which may be made of them. To say that the irrational is a "rich spectrum of life-enhancing human possibilities" is to point directly to reinforcers. They need not be suppressed by reason; on the contrary, they may be made vastly more effective.

Intuition and Reason.   It has been said that "under behaviorist assumptions, which insisted that language was behavior, such concepts as intuition were regarded as being as unfit for scientific study as ghosts or dreams," but behaving intuitively, in the sense of behaving as the effect of unanalyzed contingencies, is the very starting point of a behavioristic analysis. A person is said to behave intuitively when he does not use reason. Instinct is sometimes a synonym: it is said to be a mistake to "attribute to logical design what is the result of blind instinct," but the reference is simply to behavior shaped by unanalyzed contingencies of reinforcement. The blind instinct of the artist is the effect of the idiosyncratic consequences of his work. It is no "betrayal of reason" to accept what artists teach us about life, nature, and society, since not to accept it would be to assert that contingencies are effective only when they have been described or formulated as rules.

It is also a mistake to reserve intuition for the effect of contingencies from which it does not seem to be possible to derive rules. To say that we "intuitively" recognize that a sentence such as "John is weak to please" is ill-formed is to imply that no rule of grammar will permit us to call the sentence well-formed, but what we intuitively recognize is that the behavior we possess by virtue of the practices of our verbal community does not include a sentence of this form, nor should we as a member of such a community respond to it in an effective way.

A person may discriminate between two objects without being able to identify the distinguishing property. The intuitive diagnoses of a physician, the intuition with which an art critic identifies a school or artist, and the intuitive skill with which some people quickly learn to find their way about a city illustrate behaviors for which no rule has yet been formulated. Science often arrives very late in analyzing contingencies. It is said, for example, that the concept of torque required nearly two hundred years to be formulated, although skillful behavior with respect to systems involving torque had long existed and could be acquired without benefit of rule in a very short time.

Faith and Reason   Faith is a matter of the strength of behavior resulting from contingencies which have not been analyzed. Orthodox creedal behavior, in the sense of behavior conforming to laws, is very different from the experiential result of a mystical experience. It has often been said, in fact, that proofs of the existence of God are detrimental to faith, because they supply reasons for a belief that would otherwise be more highly valued as intuitive.

Impulse and Deliberation. "I conceive," said Thomas Hobbes, "that when a man deliberates whether he shall do a thing or not do it, he does nothing else but consider whether it be better for himself to do it or not to do it"—whether, in short, he would be reinforced by the consequences. Deliberate behavior proceeds through an analysis of reasons; impulsive behavior is the direct effect of contingencies. Impulsive works were once called ecstatic, and carefully designed works euplastic. For the Greeks a prudent or reasonable person possessed *sōphrosynē*; it was the mark of a temperate person—that is, of a person whose behavior has been tempered by an analysis of its consequences.

Invented Reasons. The advantages gained from examining the reasons for one's behavior are perhaps responsible for the tendency to construct reasons when none can be found. Superstitious behavior, for example, is the product of adventitious contingencies of reinforcement which are in no ordinary sense reasonable. No rule can be derived from the contingencies. Nevertheless, the behavior may be strong. Asked, "Why are you doing that?" a superstitious person is likely to invent an answer. The ritualistic practices of a whole culture have led to the elaborate answers found in myths. In many countries rain is a reinforcing event, and it leads to a wide range of superstitious behaviors, including rain dancing. The explanation given for a rain dance might be that it pleases the person, force, or spirit that brings rain.

(Superstitious behavior has, however, its reasons. A reinforcer has an effect even though the behavior it follows does not produce it. It has been shown in lower organisms that the intermittent presentation of a noncontingent reinforcer selects and maintains a response "for accidental reasons." The history of mythology supplies many comparable examples in human subjects.)

REASONING

II: DEDUCTION

It is not the object of a behavioral analysis to say what induction is. Like reasoning or inference, the term does not usefully describe any single behavioral process. Nevertheless, finding, offering, or inventing reasons loosely defines a field which may be profitably analyzed. A pigeon pecks a disk and is reinforced when the disk is red but not when it is green; it then stops pecking when the disk is green. We do not need to say that it has drawn the inference that green disks are not worth pecking. A baseball aficionado goes to the ball park on clear days but not when it is raining heavily. We do not need to say that on a given rainy day he infers that no game will be played. If he is planning to watch a televised game played in another city and hears that it is raining there, he may not turn on his television set, but we have no reason to say that he has inferred that a game will not be played. We need a separate term only to describe the deriving of a rule from the contingencies. The pigeon cannot do this, but the aficionado can "reason from particulars to generals" in saying, "Baseball is not played in heavy rain."

Deduction, as reasoning from generals to particulars, is also not a process requiring a behavioral analysis, but there is a field having to do with the control exerted by rules which needs attention. If someone who knows nothing about baseball is told that games are never played in heavy rain and that it is raining heavily, what behavioral process or processes will keep him from going to the ball park or will lead him to say that no game will be played? It is tempting to make a rough distinction between induction as the deriving of rules and deduction as the applying of rules, but this would be to overlook the fact that deduction is often a matter of deriving new rules from old, particularly from a consideration of certain key terms, such as "all," "some," "no," "if," and "or," where the discovery of rules for deriving new rules from old would seem to be an example of induction.

This is not the place for a survey of reasoning. I am simply trying to suggest the kinds of behavioral processes to be found in these traditional fields. It has often been pointed out that a logical or mathematical formulation follows a great intellectual achievement rather than produces it. It has been said that

> Newton could hold a problem in his mind for hours and days and weeks until it surrendered to him its secret. Then, being a supreme mathematical technician, he could dress it up, how you will, for the purposes of exposition, but it was his intuition which was preeminently extraordinary—"so happy in his conjectures," said de Morgan "as to seem to know more than he could possibly have any means of proving."

The extraction of rules was evidently a secondary stage. It is a much more explicit stage, however, and therefore more likely to be analyzed by logicians or mathematicians. The initial "intuitive" stage, which falls to the lot of the behaviorist, is far more refractory. There is nothing to be done about this; it is admittedly a difficult field. A first step, however, is to acknowledge its nature. We gain nothing by attributing Newton's achievement to intuition or happy conjecture.

Truth. The truth of a statement of fact is limited by the sources of the behavior of the speaker, the control exerted by the current setting, the effects of similar settings in the past, the effects upon the listener leading to precision or to exaggeration or falsification, and so on. There is no way in which a verbal description of a setting can be absolutely true. A scientific law is derived from possibly many episodes of this sort, but it is similarly limited by the repertoires of the scientists involved. The verbal community of the scientist maintains special sanctions in an effort to guarantee validity and objectivity, but, again, there can be no absolute. No deduction from a rule or law can therefore be absolutely true. Absolute truth can be found, if at all, only in rules derived from rules, and here it is mere tautology.

Knowing

We say that a newborn baby knows how to cry, suckle, and sneeze. We say that a child knows how to walk and how to ride a tricycle. The evidence is simply that the baby and child exhibit the behavior specified. Moving from verb to noun, we say that they possess knowledge, and the evidence is that they possess behavior. It is in this sense that we say that people thirst for, pursue, and acquire knowledge.

But this brings us at once to the question of what it means to possess behavior. We saw in Chapter 4 that to say that a response is emitted does not imply that it has been inside the organism. Behavior exists only when it is being executed. Its execution requires a physiological system, including effectors and receptors, nerves, and a brain. The system was changed when the behavior was acquired, and it is the changed system which is "possessed." The behavior it mediates may or may not be visible at any given moment. There are parallels in other parts of biology. An organism "possesses" a system of immune reactions in the sense that it

137

responds to invading organisms in a special way, but its responses are not in existence until it is being invaded. It is often useful to speak of a repertoire of behavior which, like the repertoire of a musician or a company of players, is what a person or company is capable of doing, given the right circumstances. Knowledge is possessed as a repertoire in this sense.

KINDS OF KNOWING

One meaning of "to know" is simply to be in contact with, to be intimate with. It is in this sense that a person is said to know sin, beauty, or sorrow, or a man to know a woman in the biblical sense of having carnal knowledge of her. There is an implication, of course, that behavior is changed by the contact.

We are said to know how to do something—open a window, spell "anacoluthon," solve a problem—if we can do it. If we can get from here to there, we are said to know the way. If we can recite a poem or play a piece of music without reading it, we are said to know it "by heart," a curious bit of physiologizing.

We are also said to know about things. We know algebra, Paris, Shakespeare, or Latin, not only in the sense of having had contact with a field, a place, a poet, or a language but in the sense of possessing various forms of behavior with respect to them. We know about electricity if we can work successfully, verbally or otherwise, with electrical things.

All these forms of knowing depend on a previous exposure to contingencies of reinforcement, but we are also said to have a special kind of knowledge if we can simply state instructions, directions, rules, or laws. A person may know how to operate a piece of equipment because he has read the instructions, or how to get about in a city because he has studied a map, or how to behave legally because he knows the law, although he may never have operated the equipment, visited the city, or felt the hand of the law himself. Knowledge which permits a person to describe contingencies is quite different from the knowledge identified with the behavior shaped by the contingencies. Neither form implies the other.

Pavlov's dogs have been said to know "when to salivate," but they did not salivate because they knew that the bell would be followed by food. A rat could be said to know when to press a lever to get food, but it does not press because it knows that food will be delivered. A taxi driver could be said to know a city well, but he does not get around because he possesses a cognitive map.

DOES KNOWLEDGE COME FROM EXPERIENCE?

John Locke and other British empiricists emphasized mere contact with a stimulating environment. They did not explain why a person *should* attend to the world around him, why he *should* connect (associate) two features which occurred together so that one then reminded him of the other, or why he *should* think about them at all. We saw in Chapter 5 that some of Locke's successors introduced an element of belief or will into the empirical position, but knowledge about the world is due to more than contact with a given setting, because it is due to the contingencies of reinforcement of which that setting is a part. The "experience" from which knowledge is derived consists of the full contingencies.

KNOWLEDGE AS POWER AND AS CONTEMPLATION

We do not act by putting knowledge to use; our knowledge *is* action, or at least rules for action. As such it is power, as Francis Bacon pointed out in rejecting scholasticism and its emphasis on knowing for the sake of knowing. Operant behavior is essentially the exercise of power: it has an effect on the environment. The advancement or augmentation of learning proposed by Bacon was the furthering of human behavior in the interests of the human condition, and the achievements of modern science show that he correctly foresaw its character. Nevertheless, the concern for power has recently been challenged. The West is said to have made a fetish of the control of nature. It is certainly not difficult to point to the unhappy consequences of many advances in science, but it is not clear how they can be corrected except through a further exercise of scientific power.

There is room in a behavioristic analysis for a kind of knowing short of action and hence short of power. One need not be actively behaving in order to feel or to introspectively observe certain states normally associated with behavior. To say, "I know a sea lion when I see one," is to report that one can identify a sea lion but not that one is now doing so. A response temporarily forgotten may still be claimed as knowledge, as when we say, "I can't think of it at the moment but I know it as well as I know my own name."

We also use "know" to mean "being under the control of," a condition which is not the only determiner of our behavior. When we say, "I went to the meeting knowing that X would be speaking" (where knowing could be replaced by believing, expecting, realizing, or understanding), we report that our behavior was affected by some prior indication that X would be at the meeting, but the behavior itself could not be called knowing that fact. To say, "I went *thinking* X would be there," suggests a less clear or less reliable prior indication, a distinction between thinking and knowing mentioned in Chapter 7. It has been said that "all knowing consists of hypotheses . . . regarded as proven or held very tentatively," but we are more likely to say "I think" with regard to a tentative hypothesis and to reserve "I know" for the proven case. The difference is not critical, however. The assertion "I *know* someone is hiding in this room" implies weak evidence but is nevertheless a strong response, presumably for other reasons. Similar conditions may prevail even though a remark is not made.

Much of what is called contemplative knowledge is associated with verbal behavior and with the fact that it is the listener rather than the speaker who takes action. We may speak of the power of words in affecting a listener, but the behavior of a speaker in identifying or describing something suggests a kind of knowledge divorced from practical action. Verbal behavior plays a principal role in contemplative knowledge, however, because it is well adapted for automatic reinforcement: the speaker may be his own listener. There are nonverbal behaviors having the same effect. Perceptual responses which clarify stimuli and resolve puzzlement may be automatically reinforcing. "Getting the meaning" of a difficult passage is similar. The whole world of fantasy is perceptual behavior which is automatically reinforcing, and some parts fall within the field of knowledge. Contemplation of this kind would be impossible, however, without a previous exposure to contingencies in which action is taken and differentially reinforced.

UNDERSTANDING

In a simple sense of the word, I have understood what a person says if I can repeat it correctly. In a somewhat more complex sense, I understand it if I respond appropriately. I may do so "without understanding why he says it." To understand why, I must know something about the controlling variables, about the circumstances under which I should have said it myself. I come to understand a difficult text in this sense when, by reading and rereading it, I acquire a stronger and stronger tendency to say what the text says.

Understanding sometimes means knowing reasons. If I throw a switch to put a piece of apparatus into operation and nothing happens, I may try the switch again, but my behavior quickly undergoes extinction, and I may then look to see whether the apparatus is connected with the power source, or whether a fuse is blown, or whether the starting switch is broken. In doing so, I may come to understand why it has not worked, in the sense of discovering the reasons. I have acquired understanding by analyzing the prevailing contingencies. Teachers are sometimes urged to give their students a deeper understanding of what they are learning by showing them that the rules they have memorized are descriptions of real contingencies. They are not to teach the commutative law alone; they are to show the reasons why it works.

We ourselves often acquire a deeper understanding of a rule in this sense through exposure to the natural contingencies it describes. Thus, if we have memorized a maxim and observed it, we may begin to be modified by the natural consequences. We discover, for example, that "it really is true" that procrastination is the thief of time, and we then understand the maxim in a different sense. The understanding gained by moving from rule-governed to contingency-shaped behavior is usually reinforcing, in part because the reinforcers in the latter case are less likely to be contrived and hence less likely to work in the interest of others.

We also find it reinforcing when a rule, as a description of contingencies, makes them less puzzling or more effective. If a given situation has not evoked any very useful verbal behavior, we may be reinforced by what a writer says about it if we can then respond in the same way. We understand what he says in the sense that we can now formulate the contingencies he describes more exactly or respond to them more successfully.

KNOWING AS POSSESSING INFORMATION

Information theory arose from the analysis of transmitted signals, as in a telephone line. In the field of verbal behavior it could be applied to the sound stream of speech between speaker and listener or the marks in a letter sent from writer to reader. The message has, as I have said, an apparently objective status.

Information is used in a very different way in describing individual behavior. Just as the external practice of storing and later consulting memoranda is used metaphorically to represent a supposed mental process of storing and retrieving memories, so the transmission of information from one person to another has been used metaphorically to represent the transmission of input to output (or of stimulus to response). The metaphor is at home in theories derived historically from the reflex arc, in which the environment enters (or is taken in by) the body and is processed and converted into behavior. Like stored memories or data structures, information begins as input (necessarily coded) but changes progressively until it becomes a predisposition to act. In an operant analysis, as I have pointed out, we do not need to follow the stimulus through the body or to see how it becomes a response. Neither the stimulus nor the response is ever *in* the body in any literal sense. As a form of knowledge, information can be treated more effectively as a behavioral repertoire.

It is often said that reinforcement conveys information, but this is simply to say that it makes a response not only more probable but more probable on a specific occasion. It brings a response under the control of related deprivations or aversive stimulation as well as of stimuli present at the time it occurs. Information in this sense refers to the control exercised by environmental conditions.

Information theory, with respect to the behavior of the individual, is merely a sophisticated version of copy theory, The external world is internalized, not as a photographic or phonographic reproduction, but sufficiently transduced, encoded, or otherwise modified to be more plausibly regarded as stored within the body.

THE PERSONAL KNOWLEDGE
OF THE SCIENTIST

The central question of scientific knowledge is not What is known by scientists? but What does knowing mean? The facts and laws of science are descriptions of the world— that is, of prevailing contingencies of reinforcement. They make it possible for a person to act more successfully than he could learn to do in one short lifetime or ever through direct exposure to many kinds of contingencies.

The objectivity which distinguishes rule-governed behavior from behavior generated by direct exposure to contingencies is furthered by tests of validity, proof, practices minimizing personal influences, and other parts of scientific method. Nevertheless, the corpus of science—the tables of constants, the graphs, the equations, the laws—have no power of their own. They exist only because of their effects on people. Only a living person *knows* science in the sense of acting under its control with respect to nature. But this is not to say that "every instance of knowing involves coming to terms in some way with the subjective and phenomenological." Knowledge is subjective in the trivial sense of being the behavior of a subject, but the environment, past or present, which determines the behavior lies outside the behaving person.

If action were determined by feelings or introspectively observed states of mind, it would be true, as Michael Polanyi and Percy W. Bridgman have insisted, that science is inexorably personal. As Bridgman once put it, "I must describe things *as they seem to me*. I cannot get away from myself." This is true in the sense that a scientist must behave as an individual. But if he analyzes the world around him, and if, as a result, he states facts or laws which make it possible for others to respond effectively without personal exposure to that world, then he produces something in which he himself is no longer involved. When many other scientists arrive at the same facts or laws, any personal contribution or personal participation is reduced to a minimum. What is felt or introspectively observed by those whose behavior is governed by scientific laws is very different from what is felt or introspectively observed as the result of exposure to the original contingencies.

It is absurd to suppose that science is what a scientist feels or introspectively observes. No one person can respond to more than a minuscule part of the contingencies prevailing in the world around him. If it is said instead that science is a kind of group consciousness, then we must look at how this is held together, and we shall find that what are communicated among scientists are statements of facts and rules and laws, not feelings. (The personal role of the scientist sometimes seems to be emphasized because of the apparent coldness of objective knowledge, as some religious works have continued to be transmitted by word of mouth, in spite of the invention of writing and printing, because the written form seems devoid of feeling. Spoken verbal behavior has a brief period of objectivity between speaker and listener, but it is very brief, and the joint presence of two parties gives oral communication an apparent warmth and depth which is missing from a book.)

ISMS

A philosophy, a moral climate, a class consciousness, and a spirit of the times are other intellectual possessions which fall within the field of knowledge and account for some of the large patterns of behavior characteristic of a people, a class, a period, or a culture. A person is said to act or speak as he does because he is a pragmatist, a member of the proletariat, a practitioner of the work ethic, or a behaviorist.

Terms of this sort classify behavior having identifiable consequences under given circumstances. Conflicts, such as that between empiricism and rationalism, are conflicts between contingencies, and if the history of ideas seems to show the *development* of human thought, it is not because, for example, romanticism leads to classicism and vice versa, but because the practices characteristic of one ism eventually produce conditions under which a different pattern of behavior is generated and for a time maintained.

In *Five Stages of Greek Religion,* Gilbert Murray described the change in the Roman Empire under Christianity as "a rise of asceticism, of mysticism, in a sense, of pessimism; a loss of self-confidence, of hope in this life and faith in normal human effort; a despair of patient inquiry, a cry for infallible revelation; an indifference to the welfare of the state, a conversion of the soul to God." According to Peter Gay, "He christened it a 'failure of nerve.' " "Christened" is possibly a pun, but the failure of nerve is a rather characteristic appeal to pseudophysiology, a coming down to earth after a sustained flight of mentalism. The evidence which justifies ascribing the behavior of Romans to asceticism, mysticism, pessimism, and so on should serve as well in making a few guesses about the prevailing contingencies. The ascetic is no less reinforced by delicious food, sex, and so on than others (indeed, his asceticism would scarcely be admired if he were), but his behavior is clearly under the control of other consequences—most of them probably the punitive sanctions of early Christianity. Pessimism and a loss of self-confidence, hope, and faith are, as we saw in Chapter 4, associated with a lack of strong positive reinforcement. A despair of patient inquiry suggests defective schedules of reinforcement, and a cry for infallible revelation a search for rules in lieu of contingencies which might shape behavior directly. An indifference to the welfare of the state and a conversion of the soul to God suggest a shift from governmental to religious sanctions. How much more we should know if the prevailing contingencies had been described rather than the feelings and isms generated by them!

10
The Inner World of Motivation and Emotion

We have been looking at what might be called the intellectual side of the life of the mind—one's experiences in the world in which one lives, one's inferences about the structure of that world, one's plans for dealing with it, one's intentions, purposes, ideas, and so on. I have interpreted the facts to which these expressions seem to refer as aspects of human behavior attributable to contingencies of reinforcement—or, if I may repeat, to the subtle and complex relations among three things: the situation in which behavior occurs, the behavior itself, and its consequences.

Another side of the life of the mind is said to be concerned with instincts, drives, needs, emotions, and impulsive or defensive activities, and it has attracted attention mainly for psychotherapeutic reasons. To mark this distinction the word "psyche," once applied to the intellect, now tends to be reserved for the emotional and motivational life. The two sides are not entirely unrelated. To take a very simple example, operant reinforcement brings behavior under the control of particular kinds of deprivation and aversive stimulation; in traditional terms, needs or feelings find satisfaction or expression through action upon the external environment. The intellect is sometimes said to control needs and emotions, although it may fail to do so from time to time.

PERSONALITIES

We have seen that the intellectual life of the mind has been fabricated on the pattern of life in the external world. Moved inside, the environment is converted into experience, and action into ideas, purposes, and will. Making, storing, and consulting memoranda set the pattern for the processing of memories. Techniques of solving problems become cognitive strategies. The thinking person is thus converted into the thinking mind. Something of the same sort has happened in the invention of an inner world of motivation and emotion. The person is replaced by a self or personality, perhaps by more than one. A paper on the activist youth of the 1960s, for example, calls attention to a "modal personality" of activists. It describes what young people say and do when in the company of their families, peers, and teachers, as well as when they are being "active." It is an analysis of the modal *activist,* not the modal personality.

A self or personality is at best a repertoire of behavior imparted by an organized set of contingencies. The behavior a young person acquires in the bosom of his family composes one self; the behavior he acquires in, say, the armed services composes another. The two selves may exist in the same skin without conflict until the contingencies conflict— as they may, for example, if his friends from the services visit him in his home. As Marx and many others have pointed out, the individual is born of society, and his indivisibility depends upon the coherence of the society which gives birth to him. "Fragmentation of a life" is said to follow "social disorganization in which a person has been ripped apart," fragmentation being defined as an "arrangement consciousness makes in response to an environment where respect is not forthcoming as a matter of course." But it is behavior, not consciousness, that is fragmented and ripped apart, and respect is only one of the disorganized reinforcers.

Conflicting contingencies lead to conflicting repertoires of behavior, but they are all exhibited by one body, by one member of the human species. The body that behaves in a considerate way most of the time is the same body that is occasionally callous or cruel; the body that behaves heterosexually most of the time is the same body that is occasionally homosexual. What a person is really like could mean what he would have been like if we could have seen him before his behavior was subjected to the action of an environment. We should then have known his "human nature." But genetic endowment is nothing until it has been exposed to the environment, and the exposure immediately changes it. Within limits, we may distinguish between the contributions of survival and reinforcement. When Pascal said that nature is only first habit, as habit is second nature, he could be said to have anticipated current recognition that the species acquires behavior (instincts) under contingencies of survival while the individual acquires behaviors (habits) under contingencies of reinforcement.

In Freud's great triumvirate, the ego, superego, and id represent three sets of contingencies which are almost inevitable when a person lives in a group. The id is the Judeo-Christian "Old Adam"—man's "unregenerate nature," derived from his innate susceptibilities to reinforcement, most of them almost necessarily in conflict with the interests of others. The superego—the Judeo-Christian conscience—speaks in the "still small voice" of a (usually) punitive agent representing the interests of other people. It is defined in Webster's *Third International Dictionary* as

> a major sector of the psyche that is mostly unconscious but partly conscious, that develops out of the ego by internalization or introjection in response to advice, threats, warnings, and punishment, especially by parents but also by teachers and other authority, that reflects parental conscience and the rules of society, and that serves as an aid in character formation and as a protector for the ego against overwhelming id impulses.

But it is "a major sector of the psyche" only in the sense of "a major part of human behavior," and it is mostly unconscious only because the verbal community does not teach people to observe or describe it. It is mainly the product of the punitive practices of a society which attempts to suppress the selfish behavior generated by biological reinforcers, and it may take the form of imitating society ("serving as the vicar of society") as the injunctions of parents, teachers, and others become part of its repertoire. The ego is the product of the practical contingencies in daily life, necessarily involving susceptibilities to reinforcement and the punitive contingencies arranged by other people, but displaying behavior shaped and maintained by a current environment. It is said to satisfy the id if it achieves a certain amount of biological reinforcement, and the superego if it does so without risking too much punishment. We do not need to say that these three archetypal personalities are the actors in an internal drama. The actor is the organism, which has become a person with different, possibly conflicting, repertoires as the result of different, possibly conflicting, contingencies.

Freud's analysis has seemed convincing because of its universality, but it is the environmental contingencies rather than the psyche which are invariant. The conflicts between the superego and the id, which the ego so often fails to resolve, show certain familiar patterns. In some cultures the fact that a son loves his mother and views his father as a rival is almost as characteristic of the human male as the anatomy which defines his sex, but a comparable universality is to be found among the social contingencies of reinforcement maintained by the kinds of families in such cultures. Jung's archetypal patterns and collective unconscious can be traced to either the evolution of the species or the evolution of cultural practices. "The astonishing sameness of the repressed unconscious across all recorded eras and civilizations" is the sameness of the things which reinforce people and of the behaviors which prove injurious to others. The universal features said to be characteristic of all languages are the result of universal characteristics of language communities arising from the role played by language in daily life.

LIFE IN THE PSYCHE

The life of the mind is said to require and consume psychic energy. This is simply another way of representing the probability of behavior derived from contingencies of survival or of reinforcement. Instinct is "a sum of psychic energy which imparts direction to psychological processes," in the sense that innate susceptibilities to reinforcement not only strengthen behavior but give it direction by shaping and maintaining its topography. The susceptibilities are to be traced to their survival value in the evolution of the species. Some schedules of reinforcement create "stores of energy." Others lead to its absence in abulia or depression. The "great positive forces" said to "dwell in our depths" are merely the great things we might do, given favorable circumstances.

The word "depth," common in psychoanalysis, often makes the unwarranted suggestion that an analysis is profound, but it may also be taken to refer to certain spatial features of the mind. The nineteenth-century psychologist treated consciousness as the place in which sensations could be observed, but the space occupied by the ego, superego, and id is more complex. The mind has different parts inferred from different kinds of behavior. To be of two minds about something is to have different things to do about it. The term "schizophrenia" originally meant "split mind" and is still misused in that sense. To be beside oneself is to be, for the moment, two people. Different kinds of behavior are said to be kept in different compartments of the mind. "In most human beings there is a repository of violence, but the brain throws up a barrier, a fence, to keep it in check. Secobarbital . . . may rip down this mental fence and permit violence to rush forth" (another interesting mixture of matter and mind). Music, to a well-known statesman, is "an outlet for passionate emotion," as if "opera suddenly breaks into his political life and knocks down the neat compartments between emotion and reason."

The best-known division of mind is between conscious and unconscious; repressed wishes and fears reside in the unconscious, but they may break into the conscious mind. It is often said, particularly by psychoanalysts, that behaviorism cannot deal with the unconscious. The fact is that, to begin with, it deals with nothing else. The controlling relations between behavior and genetic and environmental variables are all unconscious so long as they are not observed, and it was Freud who emphasized that they need not be observed (that is, conscious) to be effective. It requires a special verbal environment to impose consciousness on behavior by inducing a person to respond to his own body while he is behaving. If consciousness seems to have a causal effect, it is the effect of the special environment which induces self-observation.

To increase a person's consciousness of the external world is simply to bring him under more sensitive control of that world as a source of stimulation. Marx and others have tried to "throw people into a higher level of consciousness" in bringing them under the control of aspects of their environment which were previously ineffective. Drugs which alter the control are sometimes said to expand consciousness.

What behaviorism rejects is the unconscious as an agent, and of course it rejects the conscious mind as an agent, too. A biography of Mohammed asserts that "it is obvious to non-Muslims that the words which Mohammed heard . . . were dictated to him by his unconscious . . . the voice of Allah was in fact the voice of Mohammed's unconscious." But if anyone spoke, it was Mohammed himself, even though he did not observe himself doing so. It was Mohammed as a person, with a history responsible for his being Mohammed, not some fragmentary inner agent, to whom we must turn to explain the behavior.

It is often said that there is an intrapsychic life of the mind, totally independent of the physical world, in which memories evoke memories, ideas suggest ideas, and so on. Here are a few examples of the intrapsychic life of motivation and emotion: Feelings of frustration produce a sense of powerlessness, or impotence, which in turn leads to apathy or to feelings of aggression. Resentment of authority turns into a repressed murderous rage, which masks a wish to surrender. Weakened faith in the future leads to anxiety and depression, which disrupts thought processes. The drive to conform prevents a person from knowing his own fears, angers, or sense of hopelessness.

By turning to the facts on which these expressions are based, it is usually possible to identify the contingencies of reinforcement which account for the intrapsychic activities. Among the relevant facts are these: Frustration is generated by extinction, which is also often responsible for aggressive behavior. The controlling measures used by an authority make it more likely that a person will escape or counterattack, and relevant conditions may be felt as resentment;

at the same time the measures may generate compliant behavior, which is why the authorities use them. The bodily conditions associated with compliance may not be felt if the conditions associated with escape or counterattack are strong.

FREUD'S DEFENSE MECHANISMS

Life in the inner world of emotion and motivation is dramatically illustrated by the Freudian dynamisms, or defense mechanisms. They have been defined as "personality reactions by means of which an individual attempts to satisfy his emotional needs; e.g., to establish harmony among conflicting strivings: to reduce feelings of anxiety or guilt arising from wishes, thoughts, and emotions that are not acceptable." Alternative definitions may be derived from the contingencies responsible for the behavior from which the dynamisms are inferred. I shall consider three examples, using definitions from Webster's *Third International.*

Repression: "A process or mechanism of ego defense whereby wishes or impulses that are incapable of fulfillment are kept from or made inaccessible to consciousness." For "wishes or impulses" read the "probability of behavior"; for "incapable of fulfillment" read "extinguished or punished"; and for "kept from or made inaccessible to consciousness" read "not introspectively observed" in the sense of Chapter 2. We then have this: behavior which is punished becomes aversive, and by not engaging in it or not "seeing" it, a person avoids conditioned aversive stimulation. There are feelings associated with this, but the facts are accounted for by the contingencies.

The word "repression" is part of an elaborate metaphor which gives a dynamic character to the effect of punishment. When feelings cannot be expressed, pressure is said to build up until an explosion occurs. A newspaper asserts that "the frightening thing about quiet people like Bremer and Sirhan and Oswald is that there must be millions of them in the United States, holding their rage inside them until—lacking the safety valve most individuals have—they explode." But what is happening when a person "holds his rage inside him," and what is the "safety valve" through which most people let off emotional steam? The answers are to be found in the conditions under which behavior becomes very strong because it cannot be emitted.

We are often aware of a strong tendency to do or say something although an occasion is lacking; we may be "bursting with good news" but have no one to tell it to. More often, however, we do not respond because we have been punished; we have "repressed our rage" because we have been punished for "expressing it." If something happens suddenly in the manner of an explosion, it is because the situation changes. We find someone to talk to and "talk a steady stream," or our behavior becomes stronger than the incompatible behaviors which have previously displaced it. If an explosion has unwanted consequences for others, appropriate steps may be taken to prevent it. The "pressure may be reduced" by providing an environment in which behavior may be freely emitted or "impulses may be channeled into more useful outlets." "Toy guns," says a psychiatrist, "allow children to work out conflicts and ventilate some of their aggressive urges." We should say instead that they permit children to behave aggressively in unpunished ways.

Conversion: "The transformation of an unconscious conflict into a symbolically equivalent somatic symptom." One of the more dramatic manifestations of the supposed power of mental life is the production of physical illness. As an idea in the mind is said to move the muscles which express it, so nonsomatic activities in the psyche are said to affect the soma. For example, ulcers are said to be produced by an "inner-directed rage." We should say instead that the condition felt as rage is medically related to the ulcer, and that a complex social situation causes both. Similarly, when it is said that spontaneous miscarriage is due to a possibly unconscious hatred of the child or of the father, we may say instead that the condition felt as hatred is medically related to miscarriage, and that it must be attributed in turn to a complex social situation. The ulcer and the miscarriage are "symbolically equivalent" to rage and hatred in that they are associated with a high probability of working harm. Conversion does not demonstrate mind over matter; the psychic does not change the physical. Physical conditions, many of them relevant to behavior and felt in various ways, have physical (medical) effects

Sublimation: "Discharge of instinctual energy and especially that associated with pre-genital impulses through socially approved activities." For "discharge of energy through activities" read "behavior," and for "instinctual" and "associated with pre-genital impulses" read "due to certain biological reinforcers." If two forms of behavior are both reinforced and if only one of them is punished, the other is more likely to occur.

The other Freudian dynamisms or defense mechanisms may be treated in the same way. They are not psychic processes taking place in the depths of the mind, conscious or unconscious; they are the effects of contingencies of reinforcement, almost always involving punishment. At best we may say that they are ways in which a person defends himself against punishment by acquiring behavior effective in the world in which he lives (as ego), reinforced in part because of susceptibilities to reinforcement which are part of his genetic endowment (as id), and not punished by other persons or by himself (as superego).

It has been said that "inhibiting forces which oppose the discharge of tension are the immediate subject of psychology," and if this is true, it is only because inhibiting forces and the discharge of tension are figures of speech referring to punishment and reinforcement, respectively.

INNER CAUSES

An angry person may have a rapid pulse and a flushed face; his behavior may be strongly focused on the object of his anger and uncontrolled by other features of the environment; he may show a strong tendency to harm that object ("I could have killed him") or may actually harm him. He may feel much of the condition of his body at such a time and take it as the cause of his behavior, but it is in fact part of the effect for which a cause is sought. Both the behavior and the collateral conditions felt are to be explained. After all, why *did* he act *and* feel angry?

When an antecedent incitement is not easily spotted, the felt condition is likely to be assigned a more important role. A person who is angry "but does not know why" is more likely to attribute his behavior to his feelings. There does not seem to be anything else to attribute it to. A mild emotion or mood is often particularly hard to explain, and the mood itself is therefore said to be causally effective (although we must still look for the sources of the mood if we are to explain the behavior).

Bruckner reported the occasion of a creative musical act in the following way: "One day I came home and felt very sad. The thought had crossed my mind that before long the master [Wagner] would die, and then the C-sharp minor theme [of the Adagio of the Seventh Symphony] came to me." This is a straightforward statement. The thought may have "crossed his mind" as a verbal response or in some form much less easily identified. (It is not usefully identified by calling it a thought or idea.) Bruckner does not say that he then "conceived of" or "invented" or "created" the theme to express his sadness; it just "came to him." He may have thought it covertly as he might have sung it aloud or played it on the organ. We do not need to say that the theme came to him because he was feeling sad; certain circumstances (news of Wagner) produced the conditions felt as sadness *and* induced him to behave musically in a special way.

On another occasion his biographer writes: "Elated by the completion of his Seventh Symphony, Bruckner turned back to the Te Deum," but did he turn back because he was elated or because the completion of his Seventh Symphony was a highly reinforcing event strengthening the behavior involved in musical composition *and* producing the condition felt as elation? The elation one feels upon completing a difficult task is only one of the states associated with positive reinforcement. One is also said to feel pleasure (reinforcement is pleasing), satisfaction (etymologically related, as we have seen, to satiation), joy, or happiness. The conditions thus felt can scarcely be responsible for the behaviors of which they are consequences, but they are often taken to explain the behaviors which follow.

Many supposed inner causes of behavior, such as attitudes, opinions, traits of character, and philosophies, remain almost entirely inferential. That a person is pro-labor, planning to vote for a given candidate, intelligent, liberal, or pragmatic is known not from what he feels but from what he says or does. Nevertheless, terms referring to traits of character are freely used in explaining behavior. A politician continues to run for office because of "ambition," makes shady deals because of "greed," opposes measures to eliminate discrimination because of "moral callousness," holds the support of his followers because of his "leadership qualities," and so on, where no evidence of the inner causes is available except the behavior attributed to them.

So-called mental measurement has been concerned with the statistical treatment of some of these inner possessions. Repertoires can be sampled and a person rated quantitatively with respect to other persons in a group. Certain traits can be reduced to factors or vectors of mind, and it is then easy to suppose that something more than an invented cause has been discovered. But many specialists in the field have conceded that factors are classificatory schemes rather than causes and that what one can predict about behavior by measuring a mental trait is predicted from other behavior, presumably because it has similar causes.

The inner world of the psyche has lent itself to structuralist theories. The spatial features of the unconscious, preconscious, and conscious minds seem to compose a kind of topography not unlike the geography of the earth. Factor analysis has led to many dimensional representations of the mind or personality. And where there is structure, developmentalism cannot be far behind. Traits of character have been said to have "hidden propensities to growth." A person is said to pass through various stages from infancy to maturity to senescence. Erik Erikson's eight psychosocial stages of ego development are defined in terms of feelings and states of mind, but the stages are in the contingencies generating the conditions felt or introspectively observed. The child of one or two may be said to show trust versus mistrust; his behavior is reinforced mainly through the mediation of others; and consistent contingencies breed trust, while inconsistent breed mistrust. When three or four, the child shows autonomy versus doubt; he is now acting on the environment largely by himself and may or may not be successful. Failure may be mildly punished, and mild punishment generates a condition felt as shame. At four or five, the opposition is between initiative and guilt; the child moves into new contingencies, and punishment for failure may be more explicit, the condition therefore being felt as guilt rather than shame. From six to ten, industry is contrasted with inferiority; schedules of reinforcement build high or low levels of behavioral strength. According to Erikson, rule-governed behavior begins to be important at this point also. The other four stages may be analyzed in a similar way in terms of the prevailing contingencies. They are all stages in the development not of an ego but of a world.

WHY LOOK INSIDE?

The internalization of intellect is fully matched by that of the life of emotion and motivation. Turning from observed behavior to a fanciful inner world continues unabated. Sometimes it is little more than a linguistic practice. We tend to make nouns of adjectives and verbs and must then find a place for the things the nouns are said to represent. We say that a rope is strong, and before long we are speaking of its strength. We call a particular kind of strength tensile, and then explain that the rope is strong because it possesses tensile strength. The mistake is less obvious but more troublesome when matters are more complex. There is no harm in saying that a fluid possesses viscosity, or in measuring and comparing different fluids or the same fluid at different temperatures on some convenient scale. But what does viscosity mean? A sticky stuff prepared to trap birds was once made from *viscus,* Latin for mistletoe. The term came to mean "having a ropy or glutinous consistency," and viscosity "the state or quality of being ropy or glutinous." The term is useful in referring to a characteristic of a fluid, but it is nevertheless a mistake to say that a fluid flows slowly because it is viscous or possesses a high viscosity. A state or quality inferred from the behavior of a fluid begins to be taken as a cause.

Consider now a behavioral parallel. When a person has been subjected to mildly punishing consequences in walking on a slippery surface, he may walk in a manner we describe as cautious. It is then easy to say that he walks with caution or that he shows caution. There is no harm in this until we begin to say that he walks carefully because of his caution. Some people may have been born cautious in the sense that they learn very quickly to move cautiously or become excessively cautious even when not excessively punished, but the behavior at issue can usually be traced to a history of punishing consequences.

The extraordinary appeal of inner causes and the accompanying neglect of environmental histories and current setting must be due to more than a linguistic practice. I suggest that it has the appeal of the arcane, the occult, the hermetic, the magical—those mysteries which have held so important a position in the history of human thought. It is the appeal of an apparently inexplicable power, in a world which seems to lie beyond the senses and the reach of reason. It is the appeal still enjoyed by astrology, numerology, parapsychology, and psychical research.

Abstract nouns lead the reader into the depths. "Liberality among the rich," said Nietzsche, "is often only a kind of timidity." There is something "deep" in that maxim which is missing in a simple description of the behavior: "Rich people give not to please but to appease." Explanations in depth are common in historical writing. The Romans conquered the Etruscans and were astonished at their spoils of war. Later they got even more from Carthage. This is said to have had the following effect: "Covetousness and greed, restrained within the Roman community by ancient rules of behavior, having once been let loose upon the foreigner, could no longer be restrained at home." We might move from traits of character to contingencies of reinforcement by saying that the behavior of taking the property of others, strongly reinforced and unpunished in warfare, became too strong to be seriously affected by the punitive sanctions implied in "ancient rules of behavior." But the letting loose of covetousness and greed seems to go to the heart of the problem, where the mere contingencies remain on the surface.

The theater and the novel would probably not survive if the dramatist and novelist stayed out of the depths. In *The Portrait of a Lady,* the young Ralph Touchett develops tuberculosis and must remain inactive for a long time. This does not bother him, however, because he has never been strongly inclined to do anything. But that is too superficial a statement for Henry James, who puts it this way: "A secret hoard of indifference . . . came to his aid and helped to reconcile him to sacrifice."

Asked whether he was not concerned with his own safety during a trip to the moon, an astronaut replied that "astronauts do feel concern, but long and arduous training programs build the confidence needed to offset this concern." The statement that a feeling of confidence offsets the feeling of concern is seemingly more profound than that one feels concern when one does not know what to do and that one learns what to do in a training program.

To say that the "central pathology of our day is a failure of will, which brought psychoanalysis into being" seems more profound than to say that in the world of our day very little behavior is positively reinforced and much is punished and that psychoanalysis came into being to arrange better contingencies. To say that the Industrial Revolution in England improved the material condition of the working classes but "destroyed craftsmanship and the intelligent joy of man in his daily work" by alienating (separating) him from the end product of his labor seems more profound than to say that it destroyed the naturally reinforcing consequences of making things, for which the contrived reinforcers of wages were a poor substitute.

The reaction of a worker to a welfare chiseler appears to depend on a history of social contingencies, common in Western cultures, in which shirkers are punished by workers, the latter possibly feeling a condition called resentment. In one analysis of the effects of a chiseler on a worker, "work" becomes "sacrifice," which is said to be a "voluntary virtue, a meaning the sacrificer has created out of the material circumstances of his life." The refusal of the welfare chiseler to make sacrifices then "calls into question the meaning of (the worker's) act of self-abnegation" and makes that "willed, created meaning vulnerable." An elaborate psychic operation involving sacrifice, meaning, virtue, volition, self-abnegation, and will has the kind of prestige accorded the medieval sorcerer, a prestige denied to the behaviorist, who simply reports a set of social contingencies.

To take one other example, the position of the black minority in America has been described this way: When a once "largely powerless" group acquires a sense of growing power, "its members experience an intensified need for self-affirmation. Under the circumstances, collective self-glorification, found in some measure among all groups, becomes a frequent and intensified counterresponse to long-standing belittlement from without." The first step is to strike out such expressions as "sense of," "experience a need," "self-affirmation," "self-glorification," and "belittlement." A translation then reads: "When a group of people acquire power, they speak about their good qualities, and in doing so contradict what has long been said about them by others." No doubt they also feel certain states of their bodies as they do so, but they do not act because they have a *sense* of power; they act and have a sense of power because of the changes which have taken place in their environment. They do not speak well of themselves because of "collective self-glorification"; they speak well of themselves because it is reinforcing to hear themselves well spoken of, and they are especially likely to do so when they have previously not been well spoken of. The behavior at issue can be observed in a single person: "When a person is able to do so, he will speak of his good qualities in contradicting what others have said of him." There is nothing very surprising about this or very difficult, but it lacks the depth of the appeal to a need for self-affirmation and counterresponses of self-glorification.

THE USELESSNESS OF INNER CAUSES

There are, of course, reasons why a fluid flows slowly, and a molecular explanation of viscosity is a step forward. There are physiological reasons why a person behaves in a manner we call cautious; and the physiologist will, we assume, eventually tell us what they are. I must ask the reader to wait until Chapter 13 to consider whether what are felt or introspectively observed are the things which will eventually be reported and analyzed by the physiologist, but some comment on the explanations they are said to supply may be appropriate here.

The exploration of the emotional and motivational life of the mind has been described as one of the great achievements in the history of human thought, but it is possible that it has been one of the great disasters. In its search for internal explanation, supported by the false sense of cause associated with feelings and introspective observations, mentalism has obscured the environmental antecedents which would have led to a much more effective analysis. To argue that "minds kill, not guns" may be simply to insist that we shall not control assassins by making guns unavailable, but other means of control will be neglected so long as we accept the explanation that minds kill. The objection to the inner workings of the mind is not that they are not open to inspection but that they have stood in the way of the inspection of more important things.

The psyche, like the mind, is a metaphor which is made plausible by the seeming relevance of what a person feels or introspectively observes but which is destined to remain forever in the depths. By contrast, the environment is usually accessible. We need to know a great deal more about complex contingencies of reinforcement, and it will always be hard to deal with that particular set to which any one person is exposed during his life, but at least we know how to go about finding out what we need to know.

The argonauts of the psyche have for centuries sailed the stormy seas of the mind, never in sight of their goal, revising their charts from time to time in the light of what seemed like new information, less and less sure of their way home, hopelessly lost. They have failed to find the Golden Fleece.

Their plight is suggested by the despair with which solutions are proposed for current problems. A single issue of a newspaper reported commencement addresses by three university presidents, who offered the following suggestions: (1) "The confidence and hopefulness and eagerness to proceed, which historically have been the fruits of faith, are now too frequently simply not there—or too feebly there." (2) "What this country desperately needs is a totality of outlook that will put a spiritual face upon American society." (3) "America has yet to release her moral power."

This kind of thing has been going on for centuries. It is surprising that so many intelligent people refuse to ask what is wrong.

11
The Self
and Others

It is often said that a science of behavior studies the human organism but neglects the person or self. What it neglects is a vestige of animism, a doctrine which in its crudest form held that the body was moved by one or more indwelling spirits. When the resulting behavior was disruptive, the spirit was probably a devil; when it was creative, it was a guiding genius or muse. Traces of the doctrine survive when we speak of a *personality*, of an ego in ego psychology, of an *I* who says he knows what he is going to do and uses his body to do it, or of the role a person plays as a persona in a drama, wearing his body as a costume.

In a behavioral analysis a person is an organism, a member of the human species, which has acquired a repertoire of behavior. It remains an organism to the anatomist and physiologist, but it is a person to those to whom its behavior is important. Complex contingencies of reinforcement create complex repertoires, and, as we have seen, different contingencies create different persons in the same skin, of which

167

so-called multiple personalities are only an extreme manifestation. What happens when a repertoire is acquired is the important thing. The person who asserts his freedom by saying, "*I* determine what I shall do next," is speaking of freedom in or from a current situation: the I who thus seems to have an option is the product of a history from which it is not free and which in fact determines what it will now do.

A person is not an originating agent; he is a locus, a point at which many genetic and environmental conditions come together in a joint effect. As such, he remains unquestionably unique. No one else (unless he has an identical twin) has his genetic endowment, and without exception no one else has his personal history. Hence no one else will behave in precisely the same way. We refer to the fact that there is no one like him as a person when we speak of his identity. (The Latin *idem* means same, and when asked whether someone is really so-and-so, we may reply colloquially, "The same!" or, "Himself!" or we may say that a person who complains of being annoyed by his neighbors is "the selfsame person" who annoys others.)

A number of terms describing a person and his relation to others need to be considered.

KNOWING ONESELF

In asking what a person can know about himself, we are led at once to another question: *Who* can know about *whom*? The answer is to be found in the contingencies which produce both a knowing self and a known. A distinction between two selves in the same skin is made when we say that a tennis player "gets mad at himself" because he misses an easy shot. He is angry because something has hurt him, and he has done the thing that hurt; hence he is mad at himself. He may even strike himself aggressively. A similar distinction is made in self-knowledge.

All species except man behave without knowing that they do so, and presumably this was true of man until a verbal community arose to ask about behavior and thus to generate self-descriptive behavior. Self-knowledge is of social origin, and it is useful first to the community which asks the questions. Later, it becomes important to the person himself— for example, in managing or controlling himself in ways to be discussed shortly.

Different communities generate different kinds and amounts of self-knowledge and different ways in which people explain themselves to themselves and others. Some produce the deeply introspective introverted, or inner-directed, person, others the outgoing extravert. Some produce people who act only after a careful consideration of the possible consequences, others the thoughtless and impulsive. Some communities produce people particularly aware of their reactions to art, music, or literature, others of their relations with the people around them. The questions asked by mentalistic psychologists and those asked by behaviorists naturally produce different kinds of self-knowledge. The first emphasize how a person feels about things.

There is little doubt of the historical priority of the inner search. It was what Socrates meant by "Know theyself." (That injunction appears on the wall of a Roman bath beneath a mosaic of a skeleton—an anatomical version of the self.) Montaigne spoke of "spying on himself" and of "discovering the springs which set him in motion." It is the priority enjoyed by feelings and introspectively observed states over past and present environments.

Questions about feelings tend to be closely associated with a sense of self or a self-image. They emphasize what a person *is,* his current state of being. Existentialists, phenomenologists, and humanistic psychologists have encouraged self-observation in this search for self. Yoga has been defined as a set of practices "by which the individual prepares for liberation of the self." Only the liberated self can assert, "I do what I do because of what I am," or, "What I do not do or will to do is not me." "Because I am what I am," said Diderot, "I write the kind of plays I do." Buffon put it in a well-known phrase: *"Le style, c'est l'homme."*

Psychoanalysis gives a person a clearer image of himself, mainly by inducing him to explore his feelings, and the self-knowledge it encourages is often called insight, a term close to "introspection." The patient is to learn to feel his own emotions, to acknowledge feelings associated with punished behavior, and so on.

Structure is naturally emphasized in an analysis of being, and there is a related version of developmentalism which emphasizes becoming. From the present point of view any change is in a repertoire, and it must be attributed to changing contingencies. When a change is disruptive, a person may not feel that he knows himself; he is said to experience a crisis in his identity. It is difficult to maintain an identity when conditions change, but a person may conceal from himself conflicting selves, possibly by ignoring or disguising one or more of them, or by branding one a stranger, as in explaining uncharacteristic behavior by saying, "I was not myself."

The verbal community asks, "How do you feel?" rather than, "Why do you feel that way?" because it is more likely to get an answer. It takes advantage of the available information, but it has only itself to blame if other kinds of information are not available. It has not, until recently, induced people to examine the external conditions under which they live. As the relevance of environmental history has become clearer, however, practical questions have begun to be asked, not about feelings and states of mind, but about the environment, and the answers are proving increasingly useful.

The shift from introspective to environmental evidence does not guarantee that self-knowledge will be accurate, however. We do not always observe the contingencies to which we are exposed. We may keep records of what has happened, as in a diary, but in general our information is sketchy. We are not always watching what happens as we behave, and when asked how we would behave under given circumstances, we often make a bad guess, even though we have been in similar circumstances in the past. Then, as usual, we are likely to explain the inexplicable by attributing it to genetic endowment—asserting, "I was born that way," or, "That's the kind of person I am."

It is nevertheless important to examine the reasons for one's own behavior as carefully as possible because they are essential, as I have said, to good self-management. We should not be surprised that the more we know about the behavior of others, the better we understand ourselves. It was a practical interest in the behavior of "the other one" which led to this new kind of self-knowledge. The experimental analysis of behavior, together with a special self-descriptive vocabulary derived from it, has made it possible to apply to oneself much of what has been learned about the behavior of others, including other species.

Those who seek to know themselves through an exploration of their feelings often claim an exclusive kind of knowledge. Only those who have been psychoanalyzed, for example, are said to know what psychoanalysis means, and the mystic claims experiences which cannot be communicated or known to others except through similar channels. But it may be argued as well that only those who understand an experimental analysis and its use in interpreting human behavior can understand themselves in a scientific or technological sense.

KNOWING ANOTHER PERSON

In asking why another person behaves as he does, we may also distinguish between what he feels or introspectively observes and what has happened to him. Discovering how he feels, or what he thinks, is part of learning what he is or is coming to be or becoming. A first step is to make contact with him, possibly in an "encounter" or "confrontation." In any case, it requires good "interpersonal relations" and an ability to share feelings through sympathy, a word which once meant simply "feeling with." Sensitivity training is designed to help. The observer is to become involved and, like the mathematician who is said to think intuitively because he has not taken the explicit steps which lead to a conclusion, he is to intuit the feelings of others—that is, to know them directly without necessarily being able to explain how he does so.

Nevertheless, one person does not make direct contact with the inner world of another, and so-called knowledge of another is often simply an ability to predict what he will do. Thus, how well the members of a training staff perceive (and hence know) their trainees has been said to be indicated by how well they can predict how the trainees will answer a set of questions. But we understand another person in part from his expression of feelings. Actors were once said to be able to "register" joy, sorrow, and so on with facial expressions, postures, and movements, and the audience read these expressions and hence understood the characters and their motives, presumably because it had learned to do so in real life with real people.

We can use an expression of feelings by asking how we would behave if we ourselves had the feelings thus expressed. Or we can ask what kinds of behavior a given expression has tended to accompany in the past. Thus, we predict what a person who looks angry will do not by stopping to ask what we would do if we looked angry but by remembering what people who look angry generally do. The attribution of feelings to others is called empathy. A person is said to "project his feelings" into another. When he projects them into an inanimate thing, he is obviously making a mistake, and his behavior has been called the pathetic fallacy. The "angry sea" behaves in an angry fashion, but we do not suppose that it feels angry. We merely infer that for a time it will continue to behave in an angry way. We can also be wrong when we project feelings onto other people. A person can "act bravely while feeling afraid," but he does so with different parts of his body, with different repertoires. We may be able to discover how he "really" feels by altering the contingencies. If he is acting bravely because of prevailing social contingencies in which "showing fear" is punished, we may be able to change the contingencies so that he will act as if afraid. What he *felt* was in both cases generated by certain features of the situation rather than by the behavior which simulated bravery. A person who says he *feels* brave when he is really feeling afraid is like a person who acts bravely when feeling afraid, and we can discover what he "really" feels by altering the contingencies. Psychotherapy is particularly important when the contingencies responsible for a verbal report are so powerful that the person himself does not "know that he is afraid." The therapist "helps him to discover his fear." When he acts bravely while feeling afraid, that is the kind of person he is at that moment. We do not need to assume that there is a fearful person lurking in the depths.

We mistrust reports of feelings, especially when they conflict with other evidence. A curious example was common in the early days of anesthesia, when many people resisted a major operation on the grounds that the damage done to the body was clearly associated with pain and that it was possible that the anesthetic merely blocked the expression, together with its later recollection, rather than the pain itself.

We find it easier to know what another person is feeling if he tries to communicate or convey his feelings verbally. Convey means to transport or transmit, and communicate means to make common to both speaker and listener, but what is really conveyed or made common? It is, of course, quite inadequate to say that "man translates his experience into sound waves that another person can understand—that is, so that the listener can retranslate the sounds into a comparable experience." The meaning of an expression is different for speaker and listener; the meaning for the speaker must be sought in the circumstances under which he emits a verbal response and for the listener in the response he makes to a verbal stimulus. At best the end product of communication could be said to be the fact that the listener's response is appropriate to the speaker's situation. A description of the bodily state felt by the speaker does not by itself produce a similar state to be felt by the listener. It does not make a feeling common to both.

Another technique for "communicating a feeling" is to describe a situation which arouses the same feeling. As we describe something by saying what it looks *like,* and thus enable the listener to respond to it as he has already responded to something else, so we can induce the listener to feel as we feel by describing a situation which creates a condition felt in the same way. We saw an example of this in Keats's report of how he felt on first looking into Chapman's Homer. The novelist "communicates" with the reader by describing situations which generate feelings. (The same practice is useful in "communicating ideas": an argument is developed from which the reader comes to the same conclusion as the writer.)

Terms describing private events are necessarily inexact. This is true of the world of ideas (it does not help much to be told that "a good lecturer should communicate being"), and even more specific references to "what is in the speaker's mind" are faulty. Not all contingencies can be replaced with rules, and some contingency-shaped behavior is beyond the reach of verbal description. Similarly, the most precise description of a state of feeling cannot correspond exactly to the state felt. The feelings of the mystic or the aesthete are "ineffable," and there are other feelings that can be known only by passing through a relevant history. Only one who has lived in a concentration camp can really know what "it feels like," because there is nothing like it to generate comparable feelings in others. If it is true that only those who have been psychoanalyzed can know what it feels like, then presumably there is nothing else that feels like it.

We try to discover how another person feels for many reasons. A good deal of our behavior is reinforced by its effect on others, and it is presumably more reinforcing if the effect is clear. Thus, we act to reinforce those we like or love and to avoid harming them, in part because of what they do in return. (The tendency could be innate, since there is survival value, for example, in the behavior of a mother who feeds and cares for her young and protects them from harm and who, in doing so, provides conditions which classify as positive and negative reinforcers, but social contingencies of reinforcement generate comparable behavior.) It is important that the recipient show that we have been successful, and he can do so by reporting his feelings. A person being massaged says that it feels good; a person for whom a particular piece of music is being played says that he likes it. When these "signs of feeling" are absent, we may ask or otherwise investigate how a person feels.

There may seem to be a more compelling reason for probing the feelings of others. If it is "not the behavior that counts but how a person feels about his behavior," the discovery of feelings should be the first order of business. But how a person feels about his behavior depends upon the behavior and upon the conditions of which it is a function, and we can deal with these without examining feelings. When we are helping people to act more effectively, our first task may seem to be to change how they feel and thus how they will act, but a much more effective program is to change how they act and thus, incidentally, how they feel.

In a behavioristic analysis knowing another person is simply knowing what he does, has done, or will do and the genetic endowment and past and present environments which explain why he does it. It is not an easy assignment, because many relevant facts are out of reach, and each person is indubitably unique. But our knowledge of another person is limited by accessibility, not by the nature of the facts. We cannot know all there is to know, as we cannot know all we should like to know about the worlds of physics and biology, but that does not mean that what remains unknown is of a different nature. As in other sciences, we often lack the information necessary for prediction and control and must be satisfied with interpretation, but our interpretations will have the support of the prediction and control which have been possible under other conditions.

We can know another person in the other senses of knowing discussed in Chapter 9. We understand other people short of taking action, and the mere perception of others must be included among our responses to them. All this depends upon what others do, much more than upon what they feel or report they feel.

MANAGING ONESELF

Self-management raises the same question as self-knowledge: Who are the managing and managed selves? And again the answer is that they are repertoires of behavior. The intellectual self-management discussed in Chapter 7 is a matter of changing a situation until a response appears which solves a problem, the problem-solving repertoire making the repertoire containing the successful solution more effective. The two repertoires are more easily distinguished in ethical self-management. The managed self is composed of what is significantly called selfish behavior— the product of the biological reinforcers to which the species has been made sensitive through natural selection. The managing self, on the other hand, is set up mainly by the social environment, which has *its* selfish reasons for teaching a person to alter his behavior in such a way that it becomes less aversive and possibly more reinforcing to others. Self management is often represented as the direct manipulation of feelings and states of mind. A person is to change his mind, use his will power, stop feeling anxious, and love his enemies. What he actually does is change the world in which he lives. In both intellectual and ethical self-management he analyzes contingencies and may extract and apply rules. But very little self-management in this sense could be learned in one lifetime. Hence the value of folk wisdom, rules of thumb, proverbs, maxims, and other rules to be followed to adjust more expediently to the contingencies they describe. An illuminating example is the Golden Rule. It would be impossible to construct a table of commandments applicable to all the things people do which affect others, but to discover whether a *particular* act is likely to be punished because it affects others aversively the individual is enjoined to examine the effect on himself. This is the early and negative form of the Rule, but he may also look for reinforcing effects. The joint Rule tells him to avoid acting if the effect would be aversive to himself and to act if the effect would be reinforcing. Note that he is not asked to examine his putative *feelings* or to predict the feelings his behavior would induce in others; he is to see whether it is the kind of consequence he would act to achieve. In examining such an effect on himself (as by recalling his history or generalizing from it), he may well respond to conditions of his own body rather than to the changes induced in his behavior. The conditions felt in association with reinforcers are salient; but self-management is concerned with consequences, many of them due to action taken by others, and the rule is more exactly applied if a person recollects not what he has felt but what he has done when others have treated him in a given way.

Some well-known techniques of self-management are designed to bring a person's history into play in offsetting an aversive effect. For example, drinking alcoholic beverages often has two opposing consequences: an immediate reinforcement and a deferred punishment. After being punished, a person may "resolve" not to drink again. A resolution is a kind of self-made rule, designed to extend the effect of punishment into the future, but on a later occasion the immediate reinforcing effect may still take over. Recalling the resolution is a gesture of self-management, though possibly ineffective. Avoiding situations in which one is likely to drink ("avoiding temptation") is possibly more effective.

A common technique of intellectual self-management is to arrange a situation—for example, a study or studio—in which there is little to interfere with a given kind of behavior. The cloister and the hermitage have similar effects in ethical self-management. The artist who paints photographically is under the powerful control of his model, but if he can bring his personal history into play, his work will show a kind of generality, because it will be less closely tied to one situation. He will have "extracted the essentials" by attenuating the control exerted by the current setting. The same principle underlies the practice of Zen, in which the archer, for example, learns to minimize the particular features of a single instance. Both the artist and the archer are said to "transcend" the immediate situation; they become "detached" from it.

Personal history asserts itself in self-control or self-management in other ways. The individual who refuses to "go under" in a concentration camp, who is not "broken" by efforts made to demean or destroy his dignity or identity, has transcended his current environment. To say that he is able to inject a different meaning into that environment is simply to say that he is under the more powerful control of his history.

The goal of self-management is often called self-fulfillment or self-actualization. Fulfillment seems to be concerned with achievement, with avoiding restraints and discovering positive reinforcers. Actualization seems to have more to do with maximizing genetic and environmental history in order to free a person from immediate settings. In both cases the emphasis is clearly upon the here and now, on being or well-being or momentary becoming.

A good deal of interest has recently been shown in the so-called self-control of autonomic responses, such as changes in heart rate, or blood pressure, or blushing, or sweating. These reflex mechanisms have been called involuntary, and as we saw in Chapter 4, this would seem to set them apart from operant behavior, but the conditions needed for operant conditioning can be arranged. Autonomic behavior is usually concerned with the internal economy, and there have been few effects on the environment which would make operant conditioning relevant, but a conspicuous indicator that a response is occurring can be set up, and operant contingencies can thus be established. A given heart rate, for example, can turn on a light, which is then followed by a reinforcing consequence. But slowing or speeding the pulse is no more self-control than slowing or speeding one's stride when walking. The only difference is that the pulse is not *normally* followed by reinforcing consequences which bring it under operant control. Consequences are sometimes made more conspicuous in the operant conditioning of skeletal muscles. Thus, it is easier to learn to wiggle one's ears by looking in a mirror to improve feedback, and slight movements of a partially paralyzed limb are sometimes amplified for the same reason.

One can control one's pulse to some extent by behaving in ways which affect it, speeding the heart rate by exercising violently and slowing it by relaxing. The direct operant control of autonomic behavior can be demonstrated only when indirect control is eliminated. Many years ago a colleague and I tried to reinforce changes in the volume of the forearm, presumably reflecting the relaxation of blood vessels. One of us would put his forearm in a water-filled jacket (called a plethysmograph), the volume of which was indicated on a dial. We found that we could move the dial in a direction which indicated that the volume of our arm had increased, but we later discovered that we were doing so by breathing more and more deeply. By holding a greater amount of residual air in our lungs, we were squeezing blood into the arm. There are ways in which these mediating responses can be eliminated, and the pure operant control of autonomic behavior may be possible. It is not, however, the self-management with which we are here concerned.

When techniques of self-management have been learned, the instructional contingencies maintained by the verbal community may no longer be needed. Behavior resulting from good self-management is more effective and hence generously reinforced in other ways. It is possible that a much more precise kind of control may begin to be exerted by private effects, in which case the problem of privacy faced by the verbal community is surmounted. Self-management then becomes as automatic in its dependence on private stimuli as the skilled movements of an acrobat, but although these contingencies may lead to effective private self-stimulation, they do not lead to self-knowledge. We may be as unconscious of the stimuli we use in self-management as of those we use in executing a handspring.

MANAGING ANOTHER PERSON

One person manages another in the sense in which he manages himself. He does not do so by changing feelings or states of mind. The Greek gods were said to change behavior by giving men and women mental states, such as pride, mental confusion, or courage, but no one has been successful in doing so since. One person changes the behavior of another by changing the world in which he lives. In doing so, he no doubt changes what the other person feels or introspectively observes.

Operant Conditioning. Everything we know about operant conditioning is relevant to making behavior more or less likely to occur upon a given occasion. This is the traditional field of rewards and punishments, but much sharper distinctions can be made in taking advantage of what we know about contingencies of reinforcement. Unfortunately, the reinforcers most often used are negative: governmental and religious control is based mainly on the threat of punishment ("power"), and noninstitutional practices are often of the same sort. Among positive reinforcers are the goods and money of economic control in agriculture, trade, and industry and, less formally, in daily life ("wealth" or "privilege"). Interpersonal contact is frequently a matter of approval ("prestige") or censure, some forms of which are probably effective for genetic reasons ("The desire for approbation is perhaps the most deeply seated instinct of civilized man"), but which usually derive their power from their exchange with other reinforcers.

In traditional terms, one person arranges positive or negative contingencies in order to create interests, provide encouragement, instill incentives or purposes, or raise consciousness in another person. In doing so, he brings him under the control of various features of his environment. He discontinues reinforcement in order to dissuade or discourage. He uses reinforcers derived from deferred consequences to "give a person something to look forward to." In doing so, he need not promote self-knowledge, but an increase in self-knowledge is relevant ("We must make the actual pressure more pressing by adding to it the consciousness of pressure").

Describing Contingencies. Arranging contingencies of operant reinforcement is often confused with describing them. The distinction is as important as that between contingency-shaped and rule-governed behavior. When we warn a person by saying, "Come inside. It is going to rain," or by putting up a sign at an intersection reading, "Stop," we describe behavior (coming in or stopping) and identify or imply relevant consequences. We do not necessarily arrange the contingencies. A stop sign may simply indicate the kind of intersection at which drivers are likely to have trouble, as the sign "Thin Ice" beside a pond deters the skater without threatening punitive action by the authorities. But contrived aversive consequences are usually added. The child who stays out when told to come in will not only get wet, he will be punished for disobedience. The driver who does not stop at the intersection will not only run the risk of an accident, he will get a ticket. (The sign will be particularly effective if a punisher—a policeman—is visible.)

A warning, like the rules discussed in Chapter 8, gives explicit reasons in the form of a (possibly incomplete) description of contingencies. A person who responds because of a warning is behaving rationally, in the sense of applying a rule, and this is particularly likely to be said if, though he may have learned to respond because of past warnings, he does so now because he has analyzed the situation and, so to speak, warned himself. He describes his own behavior and the contingencies responsible for it and as a result is more likely to behave in an appropriate way on future occasions. The law makes an important point of this; the person who has weighed the consequences of his action, who knows the effect his behavior will have, is especially subject to punishment.

We also talk about consequences—we supply reasons—when we exhort a person to act or urge or persuade him to act. To urge is to make more urgent by adding conditioned aversive stimuli; to persuade is to add stimuli which form part of an occasion for positive reinforcement. A more explicit kind of rule is a contract. A labor contract specifies among other things what a worker is to do and how much he is to be paid. A contract is put in force when children are told that if they behave well, they will get a treat. The worker and the child may then behave in order to be paid or treated, respectively, but the behavior may be weak. The rule may have to be supplemented by additional contingencies, such as a supervisor's threat of discharge or repeated signs of disapproval from a parent.

Emotional and Motivational Measures. When we are in a position to do a person good—that is, do something he calls good—we can make that something contingent on a given topography of behavior, which is then strengthened, and we can bring behavior under the control of a given stimulus. If we "do good" without respecting any contingent relation, we may satiate a person and in doing so reduce both the probability that he will engage in behavior reinforced by that good and his susceptibility to further reinforcement by it. We may also create an emotional disposition to do good to us. Contrariwise, by withholding the good, we may extinguish any behavior which has been reinforced by it, but if we withhold without respect to what is being done, we create a state of deprivation in which behavior reinforced by that good is strong and in which the good is highly reinforcing, and we create an emotional disposition to harm us. We ourselves and the object of our attention may feel or introspectively observe many relevant states of our bodies, but the management of the contingencies is the effective step.

A number of familiar fields of management may be briefly discussed.

Teaching. Everyone has suffered, and unfortunately is continuing to suffer, from mentalistic theories of learning in education. It is a field in which the goal seems to be obviously a matter of changing minds, attitudes, feelings, motives, and so on, and the Establishment is therefore particularly resistant to change. Yet the point of education can be stated in behavioral terms: a teacher arranges contingencies under which the student acquires behavior which will be useful to him under other contingencies later on. The instructional contingencies must be contrived; there is no way out of this. The teacher cannot bring enough of the real life of the student into the classroom to build behavior appropriate to the contingencies he will encounter later. The behaviors to be constructed in advance are as much a matter of productive thinking and creativity as of plain facts and skills.

Here is a sample of what is standing in the way of effective education: It is said that "attitudes expressed in the structure of school systems affect the cognitive and creative potential of virtually every child, as do the feelings and personalities of teachers and their supervisors." The "attitudes expressed in the structure of school systems" presumably represent the behavior of designing and constructing schools and instructional programs; the "feelings and personalities of teachers and their supervisors" are presumably inferred from their behaviors; and the things which "affect the cognitive and creative potential" of a child are presumably the conditions under which the child acquires the kinds of behavior discussed in Chapter 7. A translation reads: "The intellectual and creative behavior of a child is changed by the school to which he goes, its instructional programs, and the behavior of his teachers and supervisors." This lacks the profundity of the original, but profundity here is certainly obscurity, and the translation has the merit of telling us where to begin to do something about teaching.

Education covers the behavior of a child or person over

a period of many years, and the principles of developmentalism are therefore particularly troublesome. The metaphor of growth begins in the "kindergarten" and continues into "higher" education, diverting attention from the contingencies responsible for changes in the students' behavior.

Helping. Psychotherapy has been much more explicitly committed to mentalistic systems than has education. The illness which is the object of therapy is called mental, and we have already examined Freud's mental apparatus and a few intrapsychic processes said to be disturbed or deranged in the mentally ill. What is wrong is usually explored in the realm of feelings. (At one time it was suggested that the psychiatrist should take LSD in order to discover what it feels like to be mentally disturbed.)

Measures taken to change feelings—as in "developing the ego" or "building a vital sense of self"—work by con structing contingencies of reinforcement, by advising a patient where favorable contingencies are to be found, or by supplying rules which generate behavior likely to be reinforced in his daily life. Behavior therapy is often supposed to be exclusively a matter of contriving reinforcing contingencies, but it quite properly includes giving a patient warnings, advice, instructions, and rules to be followed.

When a problem calling for therapy is due to a shortage of social or intimately personal reinforcers, a solution may be difficult. It may be obvious that a person would profit from reinforcement with attention, approval, or affection, but if these are not the natural consequences of his behavior —if he does not merit attention, approval, or affection—it may not be possible to contrive the needed contingencies. Simulated attention, approval, or affection will eventually cause more problems than it solves, and even the *deliberate* use of deserved attention cheapens the coinage.

"What is needed," says Carl Rogers, "is a new concept of therapy as offering help, not control." But these are not alternatives. One can help a person by arranging an environment which exerts control, and if I am right, one cannot help a person without doing so. So-called humanistic psychologists control people if they have any effect at all, but they do not allow themselves to analyze their practices. One unfortunate result is that they cannot teach them—and may even say that teaching is wrong. "Help" points to the interests of the person helped and "control" to the interests of the controller, but before we decide that the first is good and the second bad, we should ask whether the controller is affected by his own good or the good of others. We must look at why people help others, exerting control as they do so. The culture of the therapist should lead him to act in ways which are good for the person he is helping, and the problem of those who are concerned for therapy is to generate such a culture, not to find humane therapists. But this is to anticipate the argument of the following chapter.

Governing. In the broadest sense the term should include all management, but it is usually confined to governmental and religious practices, particularly those which are punitive and which are said to build a sense of responsibility. Like duty (what is *due* or owed to others) and obligation (what one is *obliged* to pay), responsibility suggests aversive consequences, and we sometimes say that a person is responsible simply in the sense that he responds to aversive contingencies. We *hold* him responsible by maintaining such contingencies. (We hold him accountable in the more general sense of keeping an account of his behavior to see whether it meets specifications upon which escape from punishment may be contingent.) It does not follow that he *has* a responsibility; the simple fact is that certain kinds of contingencies have affected him. If they have failed to do so, it is because he is uncontrollable, not irresponsible, and the term controllability has in some quarters tended to replace that of responsibility.

Entertaining. It may be said that there is one field in which what is done is not really management, although an effect on other people is extremely important. The artist, the composer, or the writer of poetry or fiction produces something which seems to be justified solely by the fact that it is reinforcing, no attention being paid to the contingencies. (Religious art, ceremonial music, and books with a message are designed to induce action, and similar reinforcing effects are used for educational, therapeutic, and other purposes. Reinforcing pictures, furnishings, and background music are used to make stores, offices, and hotel lobbies function as conditioned reinforcers, to increase the likelihood that people will come back again. But I am speaking here of "pure" art.) At best the artist, composer, or writer acts to produce something which reinforces *him,* and he is most likely to continue to be productive when that is the case. But we must not overlook the fact that the consumer of art, music, and literature is also reinforced. One looks at pictures, goes to galleries to see them, buys them, or buys copies of them in order to look at them because one is reinforced when one does so. One plays music which is reinforcing, goes to concerts, or buys recordings. One buys and reads books. The fact is probably not entirely irrelevant to artist, composer, or writer, but even if it were, there is no reason why a behavioristic account could not list the reinforcing effects of works of art, music, and literature and deal with them as such, rather in the manner of the contemplative knowing discussed in Chapter 9. The fact that conspicuous behavior is lacking does not mean that mental life has been demonstrated.

THE SELF AND OTHERS

People used to suppose that they knew themselves better than they knew others (or than others knew them). What they meant is that they knew their own feelings and introspectively observed states better than those of others. Self-knowledge is then a matter of being in contact with oneself. When people began to discover why others behaved as they did, a different kind of self-knowledge arose, which took genetic endowment, environmental history, and current setting into account. The historical priority of self-knowledge based upon introspection gave way to knowledge of environmental contingencies.

The order of discovery was reversed in self-management. People learn rather easily to control others. A baby, for example, develops certain methods of controlling his parents when he behaves in ways leading to certain kinds of action. Children acquire techniques of controlling their peers, and they become skillful in this long before they control themselves. The early instruction they receive in changing their own feelings or introspectively observed states by exercising will power or altering emotional and motivational states is not very effective. The self-management which begins to be taught in the form of proverbs, maxims, and rules of thumb is a matter of changing the environment. The control of others, learned at an early date, comes at last to be used in self-control, and eventually a full-fledged technology of behavior leads to skillful self-management.

That it also leads to the skillful management of others raises serious problems to which we now turn.

12
The Question of Control

A scientific analysis of behavior must, I believe, assume that a person's behavior is controlled by his genetic and environmental histories rather than by the person himself as an initiating, creative agent; but no part of the behavioristic position has raised more violent objections. We cannot prove, of course, that human behavior as a whole is fully determined, but the proposition becomes more plausible as facts accumulate, and I believe that a point has been reached at which its implications must be seriously considered.

We often overlook the fact that human behavior is also a form of control. That an organism should act to control the world around it is as characteristic of life as breathing or reproduction. A person acts upon the environment, and what he achieves is essential to his survival and the survival of the species. Science and technology are merely manifestations of this essential feature of human behavior. Understanding, prediction, and explanation, as well as technological applications, exemplify the control of nature. They do not express an "attitude of domination" or a "philosophy of control." They are the inevitable results of certain behavioral processes.

We have no doubt made mistakes. We have discovered, perhaps too rapidly, more and more effective ways of controlling our world, and we have not always used them wisely, but we can no more stop controlling nature than we can stop breathing or digesting food. Control is not a passing phase. No mystic or ascetic has ever ceased to control the world around him; he controls it in order to control himself. We cannot choose a way of life in which there is no control. We can only change the controlling conditions.

COUNTERCONTROL

Organized agencies or institutions, such as governments, religions, and economic systems, and to a lesser extent educators and psychotherapists, exert a powerful and often troublesome control. It is exerted in ways which most effectively reinforce those who exert it, and unfortunately this usually means in ways which either are immediately aversive to those controlled or exploit them in the long run.

Those who are so controlled then take action. They escape from the controller—moving out of range if he is an individual, or defecting from a government, becoming an apostate from a religion, resigning, or playing truant—or they may attack in order to weaken or destroy the controlling power, as in a revolution, a reformation, a strike, or a student protest. In other words, they oppose control with countercontrol.

A condition may be reached in which these opposing forces are in equilibrium, at least temporarily, but the result is seldom an optimal solution. An incentive system may reconcile a conflict between management and labor, nations may maintain a balance of power, and governmental, religious, and educational practices may be effective just short of defection, apostasy, or truancy, but the results are by no means well-designed social environments.

ETHICS AND COMPASSION

We speak of a benevolent ruler, a devoted teacher, a compassionate therapist, and a public-spirited industrialist, as if their behavior were symptomatic of inner traits of character. When we ask why a person is benevolent, devoted, compassionate, or public-spirited, we find ourselves examining the effect his behavior has on others. (The Utilitarians referred to effects of this sort in defining utility as "that principle that approves or disapproves of every action whatsoever, according to the tendency which it appears to have to augment or diminish the happiness of the party whose interest is in question," but this was the approval or disapproval of a third party, not of the party immediately affected by the action.) The consequences responsible for benevolent, devoted, compassionate, or public-spirited behavior are forms of countercontrol, and when they are lacking, these much-admired features of behavior are lacking.

The point is illustrated by five fields in which control is not offset by countercontrol and which have therefore become classical examples of mistreatment. They are the care of the very young, of the aged, of prisoners, of psychotics, and of the retarded. It is often said that those who have these people in charge lack compassion or a sense of ethics, but the conspicuous fact is that they are not subject to strong countercontrol. The young and the aged are too weak to protest, prisoners are controlled by police power, and psychotics and retardates cannot organize or act successfully. Little or nothing is done about mistreatment unless countercontrol, usually negative, is introduced from outside.

Countercontrol is no doubt not the only reason why one person treats another person well. We might act in such a way that another person is reinforced and reinforces us in turn. The human genetic endowment may include some such tendency, as parental care of the young, for example, seems to illustrate. Darwin pointed to the survival value of altruistic behavior, in a passage I shall quote later, though only very special kinds of innate behavior seem to be involved. In any case, the way one person treats another is determined by reciprocal action. We gain nothing by turning to feelings. It is often said that people comfort the distressed, heal the sick, and feed the hungry because they sympathize with them or share their feelings, but it is the behavior with which such feelings are associated which should have had survival value and which is modified by countercontrol. We refrain from hurting others, not because we "know how it feels to be hurt," but (1) because hurting other members of the species reduces the chances that the species will survive, and (2) when we have hurt others, we ourselves have been hurt.

The classical concept of *humanitas* was defined as a set of virtues, but any feeling of virtue could be thought of as a by-product of conduct. A man who practiced *humanitas* was confident in the sense of being usually successful; he treated others well and was as a result well treated by them; he played an active part in government; and so on.

An "important determinant of moral behavior and a major component of character development" is said to be "willingness to follow rules," but a person "wills" to follow a rule because of the consequences arranged by those who state the rule and enforce it. The distinction between rule-governed and contingency-shaped behavior is missed when a test of "socialization" is said to "assess the degree to which a person has internalized the rules, values, and conventions of his society." People punished each other long before behavior was called bad or wrong and before rules were formulated, and a person may have been "socialized" by these punitive contingencies without benefit of rules.

People do begin to call behavior good or bad or right or wrong and to reinforce or punish accordingly, and rules are eventually stated which help a person conform to the practices of his community and help the community maintain the practices. A person who learns these rules and behaves by explicitly following them still has not internalized them, even when he learns to control himself and thus to adjust even more effectively to the contingencies maintained by the group. Social behavior does not require that the contingencies which generate it should be formulated in rules or, if they have been formulated, that a person should know the rules. It is extraordinarily important, however, that social practices be formulated.

We sometimes say that we acted in a given way because we knew it was right or felt that it was right, but what we feel when we behave morally or ethically depends on the contingencies responsible for our behavior. What we feel about the behavior of others depends on its effect on us; what we feel about our own behavior toward others depends on the action others take. The bodily conditions known or felt may be particularly conspicuous when the sanctions are strong. A person who has been exposed to the promise of heaven and the threat of hell may feel stronger bodily states than one whose behavior is merely approved or censured by his fellow men. But neither one acts *because* he knows or feels that his behavior is right; he acts because of the contingencies which have shaped his behavior and created the conditions he feels.

A theological question of some antiquity is this: Is man sinful because he sins, or does he sin because he is sinful? Marx raised a similar question and answered it this way: "It is not the consciousness of man that determines his existence; rather it is his social existence that determines his consciousness." William James followed suit in the field of emotion: "We do not cry because we are sad; we are sad because we cry." In all three formulations an important detail is lacking: nothing is said about what is responsible for both the state *and* the behavior. And if we are asked, "Is a person moral because he behaves morally, or does he behave morally because he is moral?" we must answer, "Neither." He behaves morally *and* we call him moral because he lives in a particular kind of environment.

Countercontrol is not too hard to explain when control is immediately aversive—for example, when it is exerted by punishment or the threat of punishment. There are presumably relevant contingencies of survival: when unable to escape, organisms which attack a predator successfully have a competitive advantage. But when the aversive consequences of control are deferred, as in exploitation, countercontrolling action is less likely. Most of those who had great wealth used it without being subject to very much countercontrol until the nineteenth century. It has been said of Hegel that he was one of the first to realize that a modern system of trade and industry had "spontaneously arisen from the workings of rational self-interest," and that law and government were now necessary, not merely to protect the society and its individual members, but to control the unlimited greed for personal wealth that new productive techniques had unleashed. This could only be done, he believed, if a general sense of decency pervaded society. A few emendations are needed. To say that trade and industry "arose from the workings of rational self-interest" is simply to say that men discovered new ways of acquiring money and goods. Their "greed" was unlimited in the sense that there was no countercontrol. Hence the need for laws restricting trade and industry, but these required legal action by injured people rather than a "general sense of decency." It is not enough to cite the behavior from which we infer a sense of decency, as it was not enough to cite the behavior from which we infer the compassion of those who have helpless people in their charge. We must look at countercontrolling contingencies.

Man has been said to be superior to the other animals because he has evolved a moral or ethical sense. "By far the most important characteristic of human beings is that we have and exercise moral judgment." But what has evolved is a social environment in which individuals behave in ways determined in part by their effects on others. Different people show different amounts and kinds of moral and ethical behavior, depending upon the extent of their exposure to such contingencies. Morals and ethics have been said to involve "attitudes toward law and government which have taken centuries in the building," but it is much more plausible to say that the behavior said to express such attitudes is generated by contingencies that have developed over the centuries. An attitude toward government as distinct from behavior can scarcely have survived for centuries; what have survived are governmental practices. Legal behavior depends on more than "an attitude of deference toward government" as the role of government depends on more than "an accomplished fact of power," and to say that "law is an achievement that needs to be renewed by understanding the sources of its strength" is to point directly to the need to understand and maintain governmental contingencies.

One of the most tragic consequences of mentalism is dramatically illustrated by those who are earnestly concerned about the plight of the world today and who see no help except in a return to morality, ethics, or a sense of decency, as personal possessions. A recent book on morals is said to show hope rather than despair because the author "perceives a growing awareness of each man for his fellows; an increasing respect for the rights of others," and he sees these as ". . . steps toward a secure world community, based on ever-widening realms of relatedness and empathy," and a pastoral letter insists that our salvation "lies in a return to Christian morals." But what is needed is a restoration of social environments in which people behave in ways called moral.

Blaming people in order to shape ethically acceptable behavior has an unfortunate result. Samuel Butler made the point in *Erewhon,* where people were blamed for physical but not moral illness. Compare two people, one of whom has been crippled by an accident, the other by an early environmental history which makes him lazy and, when criticized, mean. Both cause great inconvenience to others, but one dies a martyr, the other a scoundrel. Or compare two children—one crippled by polio, the other by a rejecting family. Both contribute little to others and cause trouble, but only one is blamed. The main difference is that only one kind of disability is correctable by punishment, and even then only occasionally. It is tempting to say that only one person in each case *could* do something about his condition, but should we not say that *we* could do something besides blaming him?

To attribute moral and ethical behavior to environmental contingencies seems to leave no room for absolutes. It suggests a kind of relativism in which what is good is whatever is called good. One objection to this is that it refers to reinforcers but not to the maintained contingencies in which they appear. We also tend to object when what another group calls good differs widely from what we call good, if our practices conflict. But an environmental account is not relativism in this sense. The "boo-hurrah theory" of ethical emotivists was an appeal to feelings sharply localized in time and place and unrelated to any apparent reasons for ethical and moral standards. Ethical and moral contingencies of reinforcement have their own consequences, to which I shall turn in a moment.

THE STRUGGLE FOR FREEDOM

Man's success in freeing himself from the irritations and dangers of his physical environment and from the punitive and exploitative aspects of his social environment has been perhaps his greatest achievement. It has left him free to develop other kinds of behavior with highly reinforcing consequences—in the sciences, arts, and social relations. At the same time it has given him the feeling of freedom, and perhaps no feeling has caused more trouble.

As I pointed out in Chapter 4, operant behavior under positive reinforcement is distinguished by the lack of any immediately antecedent event which could plausibly serve as a cause, and as a result it has been said to show the inner origination called free will. Reflex behavior has its stimulus and is therefore called involuntary, and negatively reinforced operant behavior is emitted in the presence of the aversive condition from which the behavior brings escape. Under these conditions we do not speak of what we *want* to do but of what we *have* to do to avoid or escape from punishment. We may, through an "act of will," choose to submit to punishment, but only because other consequences of which there is no immediately antecedent cause make our submission "voluntary."

The important fact is not that we feel free when we have been positively reinforced but *that we do not tend to escape or counterattack.* Feeling free is an important hallmark of a kind of control distinguished by the fact that it does not breed countercontrol. The struggle for freedom has seemed to move toward a world in which people do as they like or what they want to do, in which they enjoy the right to be left alone, in which they have been "redeemed from the tyranny of gods and governments by the growth of their free will into perfect strength and self-confidence." It would appear to be a world in which people have fulfilled themselves, have actualized themselves, and have found themselves, in the sense in which these expressions are used in existentialism, phenomenology, and Eastern mysticism. It is a world in which the control of human behavior is wrong, in which "the desire to change another person is essentially hostile." Unfortunately the feeling of being free is not a reliable indication that we have reached such a world.

The fact that positive reinforcement does not breed countercontrol has not gone unnoticed by would-be controllers, who have simply shifted to positive means. Here is an example: A government must raise money. If it does so through taxation, its citizens must pay or be punished, and they may escape from this aversive control by putting another party in power at the next election. As an alternative, the government organizes a lottery, and instead of being *forced* to pay taxes, the citizen *voluntarily* buys tickets. The result is the same: the citizens give the government money, but they feel free and do not protest in the second case. Nevertheless they are being controlled, as powerfully as by a threat of punishment, by that particularly powerful (variable-ratio) schedule of reinforcement discussed in Chapter 4, the effect of which is all too clearly shown in the behavior of the compulsive or pathological gambler.

Control is concealed when it is represented as changing minds rather than behavior. Persuasion is not always effective, but when it is, it breeds little or no countercontrol. We persuade in part by describing potentially reinforcing consequences. A well-known ecologist has discussed the possibility of making industries pay for the right to pollute air, land, and water. This requires either legislation or voluntary agreement by industry, and "in our kind of democracy" either is possible only "by persuasion, by creating a favorable climate of public opinion." Journalists and those who control the mass media must play an important role. Another appeal to persuasion led to the following comment in the London *Times*:

Now it is the majority that never had it so good, and it is democratically determined to maintain that situation. "We must persuade . . . persuade . . . persuade . . ." says Mr. Jenkins. "Our only hope is to appeal to the latent idealism of all men and women of good will." But that is evangelism, not politics. . . . It is hoped that in his subsequent speeches Mr. Jenkins will discuss the political techniques whereby the majority can be controlled.

The control of behavior is concealed or disguised in education, psychotherapy, and religion, when the role of teacher, therapist, or priest is said to be to guide, direct, or counsel, rather than to manage, and where measures which cannot be so disguised are rejected as intervention. Social proposals often carefully omit any reference to means: we need, for example, to make "better utilization of human resources," the control involved in "utilization" not being specified.

The embarrassment of those who find themselves in a position where they must recommend control is exemplified by the Declaration of Principles issued by the Stockholm Conference on the Environment held in 1971. The first principle begins, "Man has the fundamental right to freedom, equality, and adequate conditions of life, in an environment of a quality that permits a life of dignity and well-being, and he bears a solemn responsibility to protect and improve the environment for future generations." No other species has rights and responsibilities in this sense, and it is difficult to see how they could have evolved as fundamental human traits or possessions under natural selection unless we regard them as controlling and countercontrolling practices. To assert a right is to threaten action against those who are said to infringe it. Thus, we act to restrain those who force us to act (and who thereby reduce our feeling of freedom), or who take more than their share of available goods, or who foul the world in which we live.

We justify and explain our behavior when we claim the right to restrain them. Those who defend human rights point to measures to be taken against those who infringe them. The Bill of Rights, for example, protects the individual against certain kinds of legal action.

Man "bears a solemn responsibility" not to control others aversively, not to take more than a just share of goods, and not to foul the environment, in the sense that he will be criticized or punished by those who suffer if he does so. The responsibility is not a personal possession but a property of the (mainly legal) contingencies to which people are exposed. By turning from rights and responsibilities to the behaviors attributed to them or said to be justified by them, and in turning to the social (usually governmental) contingencies which shape and maintain those behaviors, we escape from a centuries-old controversy and move toward possibly effective action.

The declaration of the Stockholm conference contained twenty-six principles. The conference had no military or economic, and very little educational, power; it could only make recommendations. In the English version we find that eleven principles asserted that states, planners, policies, and so on *must* take certain kinds of action. Five asserted that they *should,* and three that they *shall.* Five simply pointed out that action is essential, and one acknowledged a sovereign right. Perhaps it would be unfair to ask more of this particular conference, but it was called to meet possibly the greatest current threat to the species, and it is clear that it made little progress because it could not accept the fact that an essential step was the restriction of certain freedoms.

THE CONTROLLING SOCIAL ENVIRONMENT

People have suffered so long and so painfully from the controls imposed upon them that it is easy to understand why they so bitterly oppose any form of control. A simple analysis of controlling practices, such as that in the preceding chapter, is likely to be attacked simply because it could be misused by controllers. But in the long run any effective countercontrol leading to the "liberation" of the individual can be achieved only by explicit design, and this must be based upon a scientific analysis of human behavior. We must surely begin with the fact that human behavior is always controlled. "Man is born free," said Rousseau, "and is everywhere in chains," but no one is less free than a newborn child, nor will he become free as he grows older His only hope is that he will come under the control of a natural and social environment in which he will make the most of his genetic endowment and in doing so most successfully pursue happiness. His family and his peers are part of that environment, and he will benefit if they behave in ethical ways. Education is another part of that environment, and he will acquire the most effective repertoire if his teachers recognize their role for what it is rather than assume that it is to leave him free to develop himself. His government is part of that environment, and it will "govern least" if it minimizes its punitive measures. He will produce what he and others need most effectively and least aversively if incentive conditions are such that he works carefully and industriously and is reinforced by what he does. All this will be possible not because those with whom he associates possess morality and a sense of ethics or decency or compassion, but because they in turn are controlled by a particular kind of social environment.

The most important contribution of a social environment —a contribution wholly abandoned in the return to a thoroughgoing individualism—has to do with the mediation of the future. The brutal prospect of overpopulation, pollution, and the exhaustion of resources has given the future a new and relatively immediate significance, but some concern for the future has, of course, long prevailed. It has been said that a hundred years ago "there were few men alive, whether Utilitarians or religious people, who then thought of the goodness of an act as being in the act itself or in the will that willed it; all was in the consequences, for their happiness tomorrow or the 'life hereafter'; both were matters of future reward." But goodness in the light of which an act may be judged is one thing; inducing people to be good or to act well "for the sake of a future consequence" is another. The important thing is that institutions last longer than individuals and arrange contingencies which take a reasonably remote future into account. The behavioral processes are illustrated by a person who works for a promised return, who plays a game in order to win, or who buys a lottery ticket. With their help, religious institutions make the prospect of an afterlife reinforcing, and governments induce people to die patriotic deaths.

We object to much of this, but the interests of institutions sometimes coincide with the interests of individuals: governments and religions sometimes induce people to behave well with respect to each other and to act together for protection and support. Proverbs and maxims, as well as explicit codes of law, strengthen behavior having deferred consequences. By himself an individual can acquire very little behavior with respect to the future in his own lifetime, but as a member of a group he profits from the social environment maintained by the group. This is a fact of the greatest importance because it leads to an answer to two basic questions: How can we call a particular instance of the control of human behavior good or bad, and who is to design and maintain controlling practices?

THE EVOLUTION OF A CULTURE

The social environment I have been referring to is usually called a culture, though a culture is often defined in other ways—as a set of customs or manners, as a system of values and ideas, as a network of communication, and so on. As a set of contingencies of reinforcement maintained by a group, possibly formulated in rules or laws, it has a clear-cut physical status, a continuing existence beyond the lives of members of the group, a changing pattern as practices are added, discarded, or modified, and, above all, power. A culture so defined *controls* the behavior of the members of the group that practices it.

It is not a monolithic thing, and we have no reason to explain it by appealing to a group mind, idea, or will. If there are indeed "seventy-three elements of culture common to every human society still existing or known to history," then there must be seventy-three practices or kinds of practices in every set of contingencies called a culture, each of which must be explained in terms of conditions prevailing before the culture emerged as such. Why do people develop a language? Why do they practice some kind of marriage? Why do they maintain moral practices and formulate them in codes? Some answers to questions of this sort are to be found in the biological characteristics of the species, others in "universal features" of the environments in which people live.

The important thing about a culture so defined is that it evolves. A practice arises as a mutation, it affects the chances that the group will solve its problems, and if the group survives, the practice survives with it. It has been selected by its contribution to the effectiveness of those who practice it. Here is another example of that subtle process called selection, and it has the same familiar features. Mutations may be random. A culture need not have been designed, and its evolution does not show a purpose.

The practices which compose a culture are a mixed bag, and some parts may be inconsistent with others or in open conflict. Our own culture is sometimes called sick, and in a sick society, man will lack a sense of identity and feelings of competence; he will see the suspension of his own thought structures . . . to enter into a more fruitful relationship with those around him as betrayal; he will approach the world of human interaction with a sense of real despair; and only when he has been through that despair and learnt to know himself will he attain as much of what is self-fulfilling as the human condition allows.

In translation: a sick society is a set of contingencies which generate disparate or conflicting behaviors suggesting more than one self, which does not generate the strong behavior with which a feeling of competence is associated, which fails to generate successful social behavior and hence leads a person to call the behavior of others betrayal, and which, supplying only infrequent reinforcement, generates the condition felt as despair. Another writer has said that our culture is "in convulsions owing to its state of value contradiction, its incorporation of opposing and conflicting values," but we may say that the values, here as elsewhere, refer to reinforcers, and that it is the contingencies of which they are a part which are opposing and conflicting.

The society will be "cured" if it can be changed in such a way that a person is generously and consistently reinforced and therefore "fulfills himself" by acquiring and exhibiting the most successful behavior of which he is capable. Better ways of teaching (introduced for whatever reason, possibly only because of immediate consequences for teacher or student) will make a more effective use of the human genetic endowment. Better incentive conditions (introduced for whatever reason, possibly only in the interests of management or labor) mean more and better goods and more enjoyable working conditions. Better ways of governing (introduced for whatever reason, possibly merely in the interests of governed or governor) mean less time wasted in personal defense and more time for other things. More interesting forms of art, music, and literature (created for whatever reason, possibly simply for the immediate reinforcement of those creating or enjoying them) mean fewer defections to other ways of life.

In a well-known passage in *The Descent of Man,* Darwin wrote:

> Obscure as is the problem of the advance of civilization, we can at least see that the nation which produced, during a lengthened period, the greatest number of highly intellectual, energetic, brave, patriotic, and benevolent men, would generally prevail over less favored nations.

The point survives when the appeal to character is corrected by speaking of "a nation which maintains a social environment in which its citizens behave in ways called intelligent, energetic, brave, patriotic, and benevolent." Darwin was speaking of the survival value of a culture.

There are remarkable similarities in natural selection, operant conditioning, and the evolution of social environments. Not only do all three dispense with a prior creative design and a prior purpose, they invoke the notion of survival as a value. What is good for the species is what makes for its survival. What is good for the individual is what promotes his well-being. What is good for a culture is what permits it to solve its problems. There are, as we have seen, other kinds of values, but they eventually take second place to survival.

The notion of evolution is misleading—and it misled both Herbert Spencer and Darwin—when it suggests that the good represented by survival will naturally work itself out. Things go wrong under all three contingencies of selection, and they may need to be put right by explicit design. Breeding practices have long represented a kind of intervention in the evolution of the species, and geneticists are now talking about changing genetic codes. The behavior of the individual is easily changed by designing new contingencies of reinforcement. New cultural practices are explicitly designed in such fields as education, psychotherapy, penology, and economic incentives.

The design of human behavior implies, of course, control, and possibly the question most often asked of the behaviorist is this: Who is to control? The question represents the age-old mistake of looking to the individual rather than to the world in which he lives. It will not be a benevolent dictator, a compassionate therapist, a devoted teacher, or a public-spirited industrialist who will design a way of life in the interests of everyone. We must look instead at the conditions under which people govern, give help, teach, and arrange incentive systems in particular ways. In other words we must look to the culture as a social environment. Will a culture evolve in which no individual will be able to accumulate vast power and use it for his own aggrandizement in ways which are harmful to others? Will a culture evolve in which individuals are not so much concerned with their own actualization and fulfillment that they do not give serious attention to the future of the culture? These questions, and many others like them, are the questions to be asked rather than *who* will control and to what *end*. No one steps outside the causal stream. No one really intervenes. Mankind has slowly but erratically created environments in which people behave more effectively and no doubt enjoy the feelings which accompany successful behavior. It is a continuing process.

13

What Is Inside the Skin?

A behavioristic analysis rests on the following assumptions: A person is first of all an organism, a member of a species and a subspecies, possessing a genetic endowment of anatomical and physiological characteristics, which are the product of the contingencies of survival to which the species has been exposed in the process of evolution. The organism becomes a person as it acquires a repertoire of behavior under the contingencies of reinforcement to which it is exposed during its lifetime. The behavior it exhibits at any moment is under the control of a current setting. It is able to acquire such a repertoire under such control because of processes of conditioning which are also part of its genetic endowment.

In the traditional mentalistic view, on the other hand, a person is a member of the human species who behaves as he does because of many internal characteristics or possessions, among them sensations, habits, intelligence, opinions, dreams, personalities, moods, decisions, fantasies, skills, percepts, thoughts, virtues, intentions, abilities, instincts, daydreams, incentives, acts of will, joy, compassion, perceptual defenses, beliefs, complexes, expectancies, urges, choice, drives, ideas, responsibilities, elation, memories, needs, wisdom, wants, a death instinct, a sense of duty, sublimation, impulses, capacities, purposes, wishes, an id, repressed fears, a sense of shame, extraversion, images, knowledge, interests, information, a superego, propositions, experiences, attitudes, conflicts, meanings, reaction formations, a will to live, consciousness, anxiety, depression, fear, reason, libido, psychic energy, reminiscences, inhibitions, and mental illnesses.

How are we to decide between these two views?

GROUNDS FOR COMPARISON

Simplicity.   We cannot say that one is simpler than the other, since references to mental states and activities make distinctions which must be recast in terms of contingencies of survival or reinforcement. It is possible, indeed, that a behavioral analysis will be more complex. Although some schedules of reinforcement, for example, produce familiar effects which have been introspectively observed and named, many yield entirely unexpected results.

Use in Control.   Accessibility is a different matter. No one has ever directly modified any of the *mental* activities or traits listed above. There is no way in which one can make contact with them. The bodily conditions felt as such can be changed surgically, electrically, or with drugs, but for most practical purposes they are changed only through the environment. When a devotee of mentalism confesses that "we have not learned much about these problems in somewhat over two thousand years of reflective thought," we may ask why reflective thought has not sooner come under suspicion. Behavior modification, although still in its infancy, has been successful, whereas mentalistic approaches continue to fail, and once the role of the environment has been made clear, its accessibility is often surprising.

Use in Prediction. A decision is perhaps more difficult if we simply want to predict behavior. What a person feels is a product of the contingencies of which his future behavior will also be a function, and there is therefore a useful connection between feelings and behavior. It would be foolish to rule out the knowledge a person has of his current condition or the uses to which it may be put. He may say that he does what he "feels like doing" without asking why he feels that way, and we may ask him to tell us what he feels like doing and use his answer without further inquiry, as we prepare for his behavior. In casual discourse the limits of accuracy noted in Chapter 2 are not necessarily serious, but we can nevertheless predict behavior more accurately if we have direct knowledge about the history to which feelings are to be traced.

Attitudes, opinions, or intelligence, as states inferred from behavior, are also useless in control, but they permit us to predict one kind of behavior from another kind known to be associated with it, presumably because of a common cause.

Use in Interpretation. When human behavior is observed under conditions which cannot be exactly described and where histories are out of reach, very little prediction or control is possible, but a behavioristic account is still more useful than a mentalistic one in interpreting what a person is doing or why he behaves as he does under such circumstances. A listener usually has no trouble in identifying the ideas a speaker is expressing, although he has no independent evidence, but if we are going to guess, it is more helpful to guess about genetic endowment and environmental history than about the feelings which have resulted from them.

How Far Back?   When a person says that he acted "because he felt like acting," we can put little faith in the "because" until we have explained why he had the feeling, but it has been objected that we must stop somewhere in following a causal chain into the past and may as well stop at the psychic level. Clearly that is what is done most of the time in mentalistic discussions, and that is why they block further inquiry. It is true that we could trace human behavior not only to the physical conditions which shape and maintain it but also to the causes of those conditions and the causes of those causes, almost *ad infinitum,* but there is no point in going back beyond the point at which effective action can be taken. That point is not to be found in the psyche, and the explanatory force of mental life has steadily declined as the promise of the environment has come to be more clearly understood.

Relation to Other Sciences.   Another question is this: Which position more readily promotes a cooperative interchange with the social sciences on the one hand and physiology on the other? Here, again, the behavioristic position seems to take first place. The social sciences were once heavily "psychologistic." Economics had its Economic Man and political science its Political Animal, but when it was recognized that the psychological properties of these creatures were obviously being invented precisely to explain the phenomena at issue, psychologism was rejected. A behavioristic formulation may be said to restore the role of the individual in social science. The result is not the "behavioralism" of political action (which, as we have seen, is a version of structuralism) but a new approach to the conditions of which economic and political behavior are functions.

The behavioral account is also close to physiology: it sets the task for the physiologist. Mentalism, on the other hand, has done a great disservice by leading physiologists on false trials in search of the neural correlates of images, memories, consciousness, and so on.

Is a Choice Necessary?   There are those who would have it both ways and who continue to call psychology the science of behavior *and* mental life. To do so is to return to that three-stage sequence in which the physical environment acts upon the organism to generate mental or psychic activities, some of which ultimately find expression in physical action. The puzzling question of how a physical event causes a mental event, which in turn causes a physical event, remains to be answered or dismissed as unanswerable (a specialist in the physiology of vision has said that "the transition from the excitations in the cortex to the subjective experience defies explanation").

The problem could be avoided if we could stay within the mental or psychic stage. In the "intrapsychic life of the mind" mental causes have mental effects, and among them are states of awareness or consciousness, and if this inner world could be observed in a purely solipsistic way, if the student of mental life had no reason to appeal to physical action, even in communicating with others, and if mental life played no disruptive role to be taken into account by the behaviorist, everyone would be satisfied. But psychology as the study of subjective phenomena, distinct from the study of objective behavior, would then not be a science and would have no reason to be.

A science of behavior must consider the place of private stimuli as physical things, and in doing so it provides an alternative account of mental life. The question, then is this: What is inside the skin, and how do we know about it? The answer is, I believe, the heart of radical behaviorism.

PHYSIOLOGY

The organism is, of course, not empty, and it cannot be adequately treated simply as a black box, but we must carefully distinguish between what is known about what is inside and what is merely inferred.

Long before Plato "discovered the mind," the Greeks were explaining behavior with a curious mixture of anatomy, physiology, and feelings. They made a great deal of the lungs, probably in part because the voice, which seemed to express feelings and ideas, needed breath, and because breathing stopped when life stopped. Both "psyche" (from the Greek) and "spirit" (from the Latin) originally meant breath. Other precursors of behavior seemed located in the heart, which beat fast in emotion and also stopped beating when a person died.

Traces of this kind of physiology have survived to the present day. We say that a person's heart is not in his work or that it has been broken in a disastrous love affair. We say that he has the guts needed to stand up to his opponent or the gall to call him a fool. When angry, he vents his spleen. He may lack the brains needed for his job, or his brains may be addled or in turmoil. At times his nerves may be shattered, frayed, stretched to the breaking point, numb, or (possibly because the word also once referred to tendons) taut or on edge. We diagnose these inner states as readily as we invent ideas and feelings, and we mix them freely. A newspaper account of the Spassky-Fischer chess match read as follows: "Spassky's blunder today could very well be the result of the shaking his nerves took in the earlier 74-move game. Obviously Spassky has not recovered, and his error today may shake his confidence even more." It does not matter whether it was his nerves or his confidence which was shaken, for the writer has invented both. In the same way cognitive psychologists frequently use "brain" and "mind" interchangeably, and all languages are said to have certain invariant features because "that is the way the brain is wired." A recent article in a scientific journal reported that "the right hemisphere [in right-handers] controls perceptual concepts; the left hemisphere gets much of the credit for the entire brain's intelligence because it is the brain's mouthpiece (language is stored there)." We are even told that "all normal highly developed brains function in such a manner as to develop natural moral ideals in response to their experiences of reality."

The science of physiology began in much the same way. Early observations of reflex action, for example, were made long before the activity of nerves could be detected. Different parts of the nervous system could be isolated, but what happened in a given part could only be inferred. This was true even in the first part of the twentieth century. The synapse analyzed by Sir Charles Sherrington was part of a conceptual nervous system, and so was the "activity of the cerebral cortex" investigated by Pavlov. A conceptual nervous system cannot, of course, be used to explain the behavior from which it is inferred.

Physiology and, particularly with respect to behavior, neurology, have of course made great progress. Electrical and chemical properties of many neural activities are now directly observed and measured. The nervous system is, however, much less accessible than behavior and environment, and the difference takes its toll. We know some of the processes which affect large blocks of behavior—sensory, motor, motivational, and emotional—but we are still far short of knowing precisely what is happening when, say, a child learns to drink from a cup, to call an object by its name, or to find the right piece of a jigsaw puzzle, as we are still far short of making changes in the nervous system as a result of which a child will do these things. It is possible that we shall never directly observe what is happening in the nervous system at the time a response occurs, because something like the Heisenberg principle may apply: any means of observing neural mediation of behavior may disturb the behavior.

A similar comparison may be made of the technological uses of behavioral and physiological science. It has recently been said that "we may be rapidly acquiring the power to modify and control the capacities and activities of men by direct intervention and manipulation of their bodies and minds," and that the biological human engineering that results will probably have profound social consequences. It is direct intervention and manipulation of the body which is most often cited today to illustrate the dangers of the control of behavior, but a much more effective control is already within reach through environmental manipulation. It is only the traditional fascination with an inner life which again leads to the neglect of the latter.

To say that "the only possible theoretical basis for the explanation of human behavior is to be found in the physiology of the brain and central nervous system," and that "the adoption of this basis necessarily leads to the disappearance of psychology as an independent science," is also to overlook the possibility of a behavioral science and of what it has to say about feelings and introspectively observed states. A similar entrapment in physiology is illustrated by the statement "If man's life is ever to be lived along entirely rational lines, free from such disturbances as war, crimes, and economic booms and depressions, he will have to find a way of increasing the size of his brain." There could scarcely be a better example of the damaging effect of the inner-directedness of physiological, as well as mentalistic, inquiry. If we are to be free from war, crimes, and economic booms and depressions, we shall have to find a better social environment.

The promise of physiology is of a different sort. New

instruments and methods will continue to be devised, and we shall eventually know much more about the *kinds* of physiological processes, chemical or electrical, which take place when a person behaves. The physiologist of the future will tell us all that can be known about what is happening inside the behaving organism. His account will be an important advance over a behavioral analysis, because the latter is necessarily "historical"—that is to say, it is confined to functional relations showing temporal gaps. Something is done today which affects the behavior of an organism tomorrow. No matter how clearly that fact can be established, a step is missing, and we must wait for the physiologist to supply it. He will be able to show how an organism is changed when exposed to contingencies of reinforcement and why the changed organism then behaves in a different way, possibly at a much later date. What he discovers cannot invalidate the laws of a science of behavior, but it will make the picture of human action more nearly complete.

MIND OR NERVOUS SYSTEM?

But is this completion of a behavioral account not precisely the objective of a mentalistic analysis? Do we not close the gap between behavior and the prior environmental history of which it is a function when we feel or otherwise introspectively observe the states of our bodies arising from that history and responsible for that behavior? Why should we bother to ask about the *nature* of what is felt or introspectively observed? Let us take advantage of the position of the individual as an observer of himself and allow him to report on the mediating linkage between behavior and its antecedent causes. I believe that that is the position of introspective psychology, psychoanalysis, and certain physicalistic theories of knowledge that are not committed to a pure solipsism.

To agree that what one feels or introspectively observes are conditions of one's own body is a step in the right direction. It is a step toward an analysis both of seeing and of seeing that one sees in purely physical terms. After substituting brain for mind, we can then move on to substituting person for brain and recast the analysis in line with the observed facts. *But what is felt or introspectively observed is not an important part of the physiology which fills the temporal gap in a historical analysis.* A severe limitation is to be seen in the organs a person uses in observing himself. After all, what are the anatomy and physiology of the inner eye? So far as we know, self-observation must be confined to the three nervous systems described in Chapter 2—an interoceptive nervous system going to the viscera, a proprioceptive nervous system going to the skeletal frame, and an exteroceptive system bringing a person mainly into contact with the world around him. These three systems arose through natural selection as the human species evolved, and they were selected because of the role they played in the internal and external economy of the organism. But self-knowledge arose much later in the history of the species, as the product of social contingencies arranged by the verbal community, and those contingencies have not been active long enough to permit the evolution of an appropriate nervous system.

Introspection has had to use whatever systems were available, and they happened to be systems which made contact only with those parts of the body that played a role in its internal and external economy. All that a person comes to know about himself with their help is just more stimuli and responses. He does not make contact with that vast nervous system that mediates his behavior. He does not because he has no nerves going to the right places. Trying to observe much of what is going on in one's own body is like trying to hear supersonic sounds or see electromagnetic radiation beyond the visible range. The brain is particularly lacking in sense organs (its responses to stimulation are not really sensing); it plays an extraordinary role in behavior but not as the object of that special behavior called knowing. We can never know through introspection what the physiologist will eventually discover with his special instruments.

The clue lies in the contingencies of survival. Just as we cannot appeal to innate endowment to explain grammatical speech, logic, or mathematics because grammar, logic, and mathematics have not been part of the human environment for a long enough time, so we must question any effort to attribute introspective self-knowledge to a nervous system especially adapted to that purpose. Verbal behavior, logic, mathematics, and *introspection* have all been built on features of the human species which had already evolved for other reasons.

THE CONCEPTUAL NERVOUS SYSTEM

The parts of the nervous system spoken of by early physiologists were, as we have seen, largely a matter of inference, the classical example being the synapse of Sherrington's *The Integrative Action of the Nervous System.* Inference has yielded to direct observation as instruments and methods have been improved, and with great gains for physiology. Another way of dealing with inference is to give it respectability by converting it into an explicit model or system. There has arisen a kind of thermodynamics of the nervous system, in which general laws or principles are established with little or no reference, direct or inferred, to the parts of the nervous system involved. Information theory and cybernetics have both contributed to this kind of speculation about what is going on inside the head. Such a model or system could apply to either the mental or physical worlds or even to both, and the problem of dualism therefore seems to be avoided. Will a model of the nervous system not serve until physiology is more advanced?

I believe the answer is no. The study of the conceptual nervous system is largely concerned with those "thought processes" discussed in Chapter 7, which, as we have seen, are real enough at the level of behavior but merely questionable metaphors when moved inside. And like the study of consciousness or the real nervous system, a model or system continues to turn attention inward, away from a genetic and personal history.

14

Summing Up

The Introduction contains twenty statements often made about behaviorism, all of them, I believe, wrong. It is time to review them in the light of the rest of this book.

1. Methodological behaviorism and certain versions of logical positivism could be said to ignore consciousness, feelings, and states of mind, but radical behaviorism does not thus "behead the organism"; it does not "sweep the problem of subjectivity under the rug"; it does not "maintain a strictly behavioristic methodology by treating reports of introspection merely as verbal behavior"; and it was not designed to "permit consciousness to atrophy." What it has to say about consciousness is this: (a) Stimulation arising inside the body plays an important part in behavior. (b) The nervous systems through which it is effective evolved because of their role in the internal and external economy of the organism. (c) In the sense in which we say that a person is conscious of his surroundings, he is conscious of

219

states or events in his body; he is under their control as stimuli. A boxer who has been "knocked unconscious" is not responding to current stimuli either within or outside his skin, and a person may continue to talk, "unconscious of the effect he is having on his listeners" if that effect is not exerting control over his behavior. Far from ignoring consciousness in this sense, a science of behavior has developed new ways of studying it. (d) A person becomes conscious in a different sense when a verbal community arranges contingencies under which he not only sees an object but sees that he is seeing it. In this special sense, consciousness or awareness is a social product. (e) Introspective knowledge of one's body—self-knowledge—is defective for two reasons: the verbal community cannot bring self-descriptive behavior under the precise control of private stimuli, and there has been no opportunity for the evolution of a nervous system which would bring some very important parts of the body under that control. (f) Within these limits self-knowledge is useful. The verbal community asks questions about private events because they are the collateral products of environmental causes, about which it can therefore make useful inferences, and self-knowledge becomes useful to the individual for similar reasons. (g) No special kind of mind stuff is assumed. A physical world generates both physical action and the physical conditions within the body to which a person responds when a verbal community arranges the necessary contingencies.

Other species are also conscious in the sense of being under stimulus control. They feel pain in the sense of responding to painful stimuli, as they see a light or hear a sound in the sense of responding appropriately, but no verbal contingencies make them conscious of pain in the sense of feeling that they are feeling, or of light or sound in the sense of seeing that they are seeing or hearing that they are hearing.

A completely independent science of subjective experience would have no more bearing on a science of behavior than a science of what people feel about fire would have on the science of combustion. Nor could experience be divorced from the physical world in the way needed to make such a science possible. Different verbal communities generate different kinds and amounts of consciousness or awareness, Eastern philosophies, psychoanalysis, experimental psychology, phenomenology, and the world of practical affairs lead to the observation of very different feelings and states of mind. An independent science of the subjective would be an independent science of verbal communities.

Must we conclude that all those who have speculated about consciousness as a form of self-knowledge—from the Greeks to the British empiricists to the phenomenologists— have wasted their time? Perhaps we must. They deserve credit for directing attention to the relation between a person and his environment (the scientific study of stimulus control in the name of sensation and perception emerged from philosophical interests of that sort), but they have directed inquiry away from antecedent events in his environmental history.

2. It is hard to understand why it is so often said that behaviorism neglects innate endowment. Watson's careless remark that he could take any healthy infant and convert him into a doctor, lawyer, artist, merchant chief, and, yes, even beggarman or thief can scarcely be responsible, because Watson himself repeatedly referred to the "hereditary and habit equipment" of people. A few behaviorists, particularly J. R. Kantor, have minimized if not denied a genetic contribution, and in their enthusiasm for what may be done through the environment, others have no doubt acted as if a genetic endowment were unimportant, but few would contend that behavior is "endlessly malleable."

Social and political issues have probably played a greater role than has been apparent, and some have recently come into the open. The view that little or nothing is due to the environment has been influential in education. Students are classified essentially as those who do not need to be taught and those who cannot be, and the doctrine of universal education is challenged on the grounds that some children are essentially unteachable. But the roles of heredity and environment are to be discovered through observation, not assigned in conformity with political beliefs. Species differ in the speeds with which they can be conditioned and in the nature and size of the repertoires they can maintain, and it is probable that people show similar inherited differences. Nevertheless, the topography or form or behavior is only rarely affected. To say that intelligence or some other ability or trait is twenty percent a matter of the environment and eighty percent a matter of genetics is not to say that twenty percent of a person's behavior is due to contingencies of reinforcement and eighty percent to genetic endowment. Raise one identical twin in China and the other in France and their verbal behavior will be completely different. (The grammars of the two languages may have certain features in common but not, as we have seen, because grammar has a genetic basis.)

3. The eliciting stimulus is a particularly clear example of environmental action and probably for that reason was the first to be discovered and formulated. The notion of a trigger which released stored behavior was suggested to Descartes by certain hydraulic devices that simulated human behavior, and simple examples were demonstrated during the nineteenth century in segments of living organisms—in decapitated salamanders, for example—by the physiologist Marshall Hall. As we have seen, Pavlov showed how stimuli might acquire the power to elicit reflex responses during the lifetime of the individual, and all this led to the ambitious program of stimulus-response psychology.

The same appealing simplicity is perhaps responsible for the fact that the reflex has retained its place in nontechnical literature as the stereotype of environmental action, as well as for the fact that behaviorism is so often said to treat behavior simply as response to stimulus. If that were the case, an organism would have much of the character of a puppet, robot, or machine. But stimuli do not *elicit* operant responses; they simply modify the probability that responses will be emitted. They do so because of the contingencies of reinforcement in which they have played a part, and they may act in combination with other conditions, possibly but not necessarily to the point at which a response occurs. This is a far different role from that of the eliciting stimulus in a reflex.

4. Human beings attend to or disregard the world in which they live. They search for things in that world. They generalize from one thing to another. They discriminate. They respond to single features or special sets of features as "abstractions" or "concepts." They solve problems by assembling, classifying, arranging, and rearranging things. They describe things and respond to their descriptions, as well as to descriptions made by others. They analyze the contingencies of reinforcement in their world and extract plans and rules which enable them to respond appropriately without direct exposure to the contingencies. They discover and use rules for deriving new rules from old. In all this, and much more, they are simply behaving, and that is true even when they are behaving covertly. Not only does a behavioral analysis not reject any of these "higher mental processes"; it has taken the lead in investigating the contingencies under which they occur. What it rejects is the assumption that comparable activities take place in the mysterious world of the mind. That assumption, it argues, is an unwarranted and dangerous metaphor.

No one can give an adequate account of much of human thinking. It is, after all, probably the most complex subject ever submitted to analysis. The great achievements of artists, composers, writers, mathematicians, and scientists are no doubt still beyond reach (in part, as I have pointed out, because leaders in these fields have been misled by mentalism into giving useless reports of their activities). No matter how defective a behavioral account may be, we must remember that mentalistic explanations explain nothing.

5. Evolutionary theory moved the purpose which seemed to be displayed by the human genetic endowment from antecedent design to subsequent selection by contingencies of survival. Operant theory moved the purpose which seemed to be displayed by human action from antecedent intention or plan to subsequent selection by contingencies of reinforcement. A person disposed to act because he has been reinforced for acting may feel the condition of his body at such a time and call it "felt purpose," but what behaviorism rejects is the causal efficacy of that feeling.

6. Contingencies of reinforcement also resemble contingencies of survival in the production of novelty. The key word in Darwin's title was "origin." Natural selection explained the origination of millions of different species on the surface of the earth, without appealing to a creative mind. In the field of human behavior the possibility arises that contingencies of reinforcement may explain a work of art or the solution to a problem in mathematics or science without appealing to a different kind of creative mind or to a trait of creativity or to the possibility that "men of genius have more creative nervous energy than lesser mortals."

In both natural selection and operant conditioning the appearance of "mutations" is crucial. Until recently, species evolved because of random changes in genes or chromosomes, but the geneticist may arrange conditions under which mutations are particularly likely to occur. We can also discover some of the sources of new forms of behavior which undergo selection by prevailing contingencies of reinforcement, and fortunately the creative artist or thinker has other ways of introducing novelties, some of which I reviewed in Chapter 7.

7. Origination is at the heart of the issue of a self or

sense of self. A member of the human species has identity, in the sense that he is one member and no other. He begins as an organism and becomes a person or self as he acquires a repertoire of behavior. He may become more than one person or self if he acquires more or less incompatible repertoires appropriate to different occasions. In self-knowledge, the knowing self is different from the known. In self-management the controlling self is different from the controlled. But all selves are the products of genetic and environmental histories. Self-knowledge and self-management are of social origin, and the selves known and managed are the products of both contingencies of survival and contingencies of reinforcement. Nothing about the position taken in this book questions the uniqueness of each member of the human species, but the uniqueness is inherent in the sources. There is no place in the scientific position for a self as a true originator or initiator of action.

8. If we dismiss the pejorative meaning of "superficial" as lacking in penetration and the honorific meaning of "deep" as being profound, then there is a grain of truth in the contention that a behavioristic analysis is superficial and does not reach the depths of the mind or personality. The thrust of such an analysis is to question the causal role of what is felt or introspectively observed within the skin and to turn instead to genetic history, environmental history, and the present setting—all of which lie outside. If behaviorism took the line of a pure structuralism, abandoning the causal role of the mind and putting nothing in its place, it would be superficial in an objectionable sense, but that is a very superficial view of what it actually does.

9. Existentialists, phenomenologists, and structuralists frequently contend that, in limiting itself to prediction and control, a science of behavior fails to grasp the essential nature or being of man. So-called humanistic psychology also deprecates prediction or control in its concern for what a person is, here and now, apart from his past or future, and

it attempts to justify itself accordingly: "The theory of evolution is not a predictive science, yet it is highly respectable and important. Hence other nonpredictive sciences—history, humanistic psychology—may be justified." But the theory of evolution is not a science at all; it is an interpretation of a very large number of facts, using several relevant sciences, among them genetics and ecology, both of which are or may be predictive and manipulative. Although, as we saw in Chapter 9, understanding, like contemplation, is a kind of knowing which often falls short of action, it is derived from conditions which lead to action. Both prediction and control are inherent in operant conditioning, but the notion is always probabilistic, and we may deal with a probability when action is not taking place. We can substitute "understanding" for "knowing" oneself or another person, but whatever the condition at a given moment, knowledge or understanding is "put to use" only when action is taken. The more thoroughly we understand the relation between human behavior and its genetic and environmental antecedents, the more clearly we understand the nature or essence of the species.

10. A review of a recent book by an English behaviorist in a well-known British publication contains the comment that "unlike behaviorists in America, the author works not with rats but with people." The reign of the white rat in the psychological laboratory ended at least a quarter of a century ago. Anything like an adequate sampling of the species of the world is out of the question, even for the field ethologist, but the experimental analysis of behavior has been extended to a fairly large number of species, among them *Homo sapiens*.

There are excellent reasons for beginning with simple cases and moving on only as the power of the analysis permits. If this means, as it seems to mean, that one begins with animals, the emphasis is no doubt upon those features which animals and people have in common. Something is gained, however, since only in this way can we be sure of what is uniquely human. It is not, as one writer contends, an error to "try to apply a system developed from limited work with animals to human society and, indeed, to the whole realm of human experience." That in the direction— from simple to complex—in which science moves. But one applies the system by removing the limits as rapidly as possible and working directly with human behavior. We are admittedly far short, as is everyone else, of an adequate account of human society or the whole realm of human experience, and it is true that "the arbitrary choice to use rats and pigeons to obtain data necessarily rules out human freedom and dignity"; it does so by definition, since rats and pigeons are not human. But if we are to analyze the issues raised by freedom and dignity, it is well to use every conceivable source of information about the underlying processes.

Even with human subjects, most of the early experiments were done where the environment could be most easily controlled, as with psychotics and retardates. (Its success there has been rather grudgingly admitted: "Based on research with animals, it works gratifyingly with those who are already mentally limited.") But normal children soon began to be studied, and then normal adults. Special problems naturally arise from the relation of the subject to the experimenter and from the long and complex history of the subject prior to the experiment, but enough has been done to suggest that the same basic processes occur in both animals and men, just as the same kind of nervous system is to be found in both. There are, of course, enormous differences in the complexity of their repertoires.

Curiously enough, the relation between animal and human behavior is sometimes said to point in the other direction. "The study of animal behavior is unique among the sciences because it begins historically and methodologically with human behavior, prescinds from human experience, and projects this experience into other animals." If this were the case, we should have to say that we are limited in animal research to those topics which can be prescinded from human experience and projected into animals. The American behaviorist Edward C. Tolman said, in fact, that he designed his experiments with animals by examining what he himself would do in a given situation, but the experimental analysis of behavior is far beyond the point at which introspection throws any light on the processes being studied. It would be a remarkable person who predicted his behavior under the contingencies arranged in a modern laboratory.

11. The objection to arguing from animals to men and women is in part an objection to extrapolating from laboratory to daily life, and the point applies as well when the organism in the laboratory is human. The setting in the laboratory is designed to control conditions. Some are held as constant as possible; others are changed in an orderly fashion. The equipment used for these purposes comes between experimenter and organism. It obviously does not promote—-it almost necessarily interferes with—the kind of personal knowledge which is said to arise from the interpersonal relations discussed in Chapter 11. The equipment is not used because it does so, even though a clinical psychologist has claimed that "experimental psychologists use their gadgets and machines to defend themselves against real involvement with their subjects." They use them for the sake of a different kind of "knowing another person."

Obviously we cannot predict or control human behavior in daily life with the precision obtained in the laboratory, but we can nevertheless use results from the laboratory to interpret behavior elsewhere. Such an interpretation of human behavior in daily life has been criticized as metascience, but all the sciences resort to something much like it. As we have just seen, the principles of genetics are used to interpret the facts of evolution, as the behavior of substances under high pressures and temperatures are used to interpret geological events in the history of the earth. What is happening in interstellar space, where control is out of the question is largely a matter of interpretation in this sense. Many technological applications pass through a stage of interpretation. We cannot study the behavior of a new type of aircraft until it has been built and flown, but it is designed and built according to principles established in the laboratory. In much the same way principles emerging from an experimental analysis of behavior have been applied in the design of education, psychotherapy, incentive systems in industry, penology, and in many other fields.

Those who argue that laboratory results cannot account for human behavior in the world at large presumably believe that they know what is happening in that world, or at least that it can be known. They are often speaking of casual impressions. But if a statement about behavior is less to be trusted in daily life than in a laboratory setting, we must certainly ask whether the impression against which it is compared is any more reliable. Those who feel that they understand what is happening in the world at large may be tested in a very simple way: let them look at the organism as it behaves in a modern experiment and tell us what they see. The contingencies currently under investigation, though extremely complex, are far less complex than those in daily life, yet it is almost impossible to discover what is going on. Those familiar with laboratory research will be more likely to look for the important things and will know what other things to ask about; they will have a better understanding of what they see. That is why they can more accurately interpret daily life. The laboratory analysis makes it possible to identify relevant variables and to disregard others which, though possibly more fascinating, nevertheless have little or no bearing on the behavior under observation. Many of the technological advances derived from the study of operant behavior have had the benefit of that kind of interpretation.

12. Those who say that a science of behavior is over-simplified and naïve usually show an oversimplified and naïve knowledge of the science, and those who claim that what it has to say is either trivial or already well known are usually unfamiliar with its actual accomplishments. To say that behavior is nothing but a response to stimuli is oversimplified. To say that people are just like rats and pigeons is naïve. To say that the science of behavior is a matter of how rats can learn to find their way in mazes or how dogs come to salivate when they hear the dinner bell is to speak of what is trivial or already familiar. A distinguished philosopher of science recently asserted that "even a behaviorist can, at the *very best*, predict that, under the given conditions a rat will take twenty to twenty-five seconds to run a maze: he will have no idea how, by specifying more and more precise experimental conditions, he could make predictions which become more and more precise— and, *in principle, precise without limit.*" This is an observation that might have been timely perhaps fifty years ago. It is not surprising that a writer who dismisses behavior modification as a matter of "gold stars and back pats" or that the editor of a newspaper who assures his readers that a demonstration of superstition in a pigeon will not explain the Twenty-third Psalm believes that a science of behavior is oversimplified.

When Freud called behaviorism naïve, he was speaking of an early version and comparing it with his own extremely involved account of the mental apparatus—an account which some of his followers have felt to be in need of simplification. Anyone who tries to make some kind of systematic order of what is said to be taking place inside the skin will necessarily come up with an account which is far from simple. But if we are to call anything oversimplified, it must be those mentalistic explanations, so readily invented on the spot, which are appealing because they seem so much simpler than the facts they are said to explain. It is easier to say that a person is suffering from anxiety than from a history of sibling rivalry to which the anxiety must eventually be attributed, as it is simpler to say that "mental retardates show reactive inhibition" than to examine the defective relation between their behavior and the environments to which they are exposed. The "complexity of mental organization" that behaviorism is said to underestimate is the complexity which arises from the effort to systematize formulations that might better be abandoned.

A science of behavior is especially vulnerable to the charge of simplification because it is hard to believe that a fairly simple principle can have vast consequences in our lives. We have learned to accept similar apparent discrepancies in other fields. We no longer find it hard to believe that a bacterium or virus can explain the devastation of a plague or that the slipping of parts of the earth's crust can explain the tragedy of a city leveled by an earthquake. But we find it much more difficult to believe that contingencies of reinforcement can really be the roots of wars, say, or—at the other extreme—of art, music, and literature.

All sciences simplify the conditions they study as far as possible, but this does not mean that they refuse to examine more complex instances as soon as they can do so profitably. The reader who has reached this point will not be inclined to call a behavioristic analysis of human behavior simple (unless he blames the complexities he has encountered on my exposition), and I may remind him that I have kept facts and principles to a bare minimum. The experimental analysis of behavior is a rigorous, extensive, and rapidly advancing branch of biology, and only those who are unaware of its scope can call it oversimplified.

As to familiarity, it is true that a scientific analysis has to some extent been anticipated in philosophy, theology, linguistics, political science, and many other fields. The importance of operant reinforcement, for example, has long been recognized in discussions of rewards, self-interest, hedonism, and Utilitarianism. Marx and Bentham have been called behaviorists because they drew attention to the environment, but they both believed that the environment acted upon consciousness, which in turn affected human action. The great essayists have extracted rules of thumb and insights very close to some implications of a scientific account. Something of the same sort has been said of almost every science; the Greeks talked about the atom and the dimension of time. The mistake is an example of structuralism: it is not what was said but *why it was said* that must be taken into account. Facts are not invented by the scientist, and facts about behavior have always been conspicuous features of the world in which people lived, but scientists quickly pass beyond the stage of folk wisdom and personal experience, and this has already happened in the experimental analysis of behavior. Very little of what is discovered in current research could be said to be familiar to anyone.

Perhaps the best evidence that a science of behavior has something new to offer is the success of its technological applications, but we should not overlook the evidence to be found in the violence with which the position is currently attacked. I doubt whether so much gunpowder would be spent on what was obviously a naïve and outmoded triviality.

13. Behaviorists are sometimes accused of idolatry; they are said to worship science and to borrow the trappings of science simply in order to look scientific. This is a fairly common criticism of all social or behavioral sciences; merely to count or measure is said to be to ape the natural sciences. But it is hard to find any sign of this in the history of the experimental analysis of behavior. Early studies used simple equipment, and the data were reported as simply as possible. The underlying assumption that behavior was orderly rather than capricious could scarcely be said to have been adopted for honorific purposes. To establish the dimensions of behavior and related variables, to insist upon prediction and

control, to use mathematics where quantification permitted —these were essential steps rather than window dressing. The armamentarium of science is much more conspicuous in information theory, cognitive psychology, cybernetics, and systems analysis, which are replete with terms like "interface," "gating," "reverberating circuits," "parameters of complexity," "overloaded channels," "and closed feedback loops" ("resurrecting purpose and freedom!"), and where mathematics becomes an end in itself in spite of the lack of an adequate dimensional analysis of the data.

If the critics who speak of the "dead hand of scientism" mean it in the literal sense of mortmain, they are presumably suggesting that there were early hopes of a science which have now been abandoned by all but a desperate few, but there is nothing in the history of the analysis of behavior to suggest a setback. In fact, compared with many other sciences, both the analysis and its technological applications have developed with unusual speed. It is true that the death of behaviorism has often been predicted and occasionally announced. A good Freudian might speak of a death wish, and a paranoid behaviorist might view the contentions I am examining as murderous in intent. But the historian, like everyone else, is well advised to turn from wishes and intentions to environmental contingencies, and a book such as this is designed to be part of the environment of those who will continue to talk about behaviorism as a living philosophy.

14. There have been many dramatic applications of operant conditioning, but very often what is done seems in retrospect to be little more than the application of common sense. Nevertheless, we have to ask why similar changes were not made before the advent of an experimental analysis. It is sometimes said that they were, and isolated instances in which something very much like a modern behavioral technology can be cited. But we may still ask why these occasional instances, scattered throughout the cen-

turies, have not become standard practice. Even the fact that a practice works or that it makes sense is often not enough to ensure its continued use, and one reason is that, temporarily at least, the wrong practices also seem to work and make sense.

The important difference is in the time at which the desirable results occur. In spite of the fact that many people find them objectionable, punishment and aversive control are still common, and for a single reason: those who use them are usually immediately reinforced; only the deferred results are objectionable. Positive reinforcement is at least equally powerful as a controlling measure, but its effects are usually at least slightly deferred. It is only when laboratory research demonstrates that positive reinforcement has worthwhile consequences that one learns to wait for them.

The disastrous results of common sense in the management of human behavior are evident in every walk of life, from international affairs to the care of a baby, and we shall continue to be inept in all these fields until a scientific analysis clarifies the advantages of a more effective technology. It will then be obvious that the results are due to more than common sense.

15. In *An Inquiry into Meaning and Truth* Bertrand Russell wrote as follows: "When the behaviorist observes the doings of animals, and decides whether these show knowledge or error, he is not thinking of himself as an animal, but as an at least hypothetically inerrant recorder of what actually happens." He was speaking of an early version of behaviorism, and even so he was not right. It would be absurd for the behaviorist to contend that he is in any way exempt from his analysis. He cannot step out of the causal stream and observe behavior from some special point of vantage, "perched on the epicycle of Mercury." In the very act of analyzing human behavior he is behaving—as, in the very act of analyzing thinking, the philosopher is thinking.

The behavior of logician, mathematician, and scientist is the most difficult part of the field of human behavior and possibly the most subtle and complex phenomenon ever submitted to a logical, mathematical, or scientific analysis, but because it has not yet been well analyzed, we should not conclude that it is a different kind of field, to be approached only with a different kind of analysis. There is no reason why we cannot ask what a logician or mathematician does as he discovers how or why new rules can be derived from old or why, if the old can be said to be true, the new must be true too. It is possible, in fact, that a behavioral analysis may yield a new kind of attack on familiar problems, such as the paradoxes or Gödel's theorem.

Scientific knowledge is verbal behavior, though not necessarily linguistic. It is a corpus of rules for effective action, and there is a special sense in which it could be "true" if it yields the most effective action possible. But rules are never the contingencies they describe; they remain descriptions and suffer the limitations inherent in verbal behavior. As I pointed out in Chapter 8, a proposition is "true" to the extent that with its help the listener responds effectively to the situation it describes. The account given by the speaker functions in lieu of the direct control by the environment which has generated it, and the listener's behavior can never exceed the behavior controlled by the situation described. The tautological truth of the logician or mathematician can be proved; it is absolute. The canons of scientific methods are designed to maximize the control exerted by the stimulus and to suppress other conditions, such as incidental effects upon the listener which lead the speaker to exaggerate or lie.

Traditional theories of knowledge run into trouble because they assume that one must think before behaving (not to mention thinking before existing, as in *Cogito, ergo sum*). No one thinks before he acts except in the sense of acting covertly before acting overtly.

It is sometimes said that to speak the truth one must be free; controlled behavior is too restricted to be judged or accepted as true, and the behaviorist who insists that all behavior is determined evidently denies that it can therefore be true at all. But one is "free to speak the truth" only with respect to a present setting. What he does in that setting is a function of antecedent conditions in which similar settings have played a part. Certainly the procedure according to which one arrives at the truth by deduction is not free; one is bound to the "laws of thought" and to other rules for deriving new rules from old. The intuitions which seem to anticipate deduction but are later deductively proved suggest a kind of freedom, but not if intuitive behavior is contingency-shaped rather than rule-governed. Induction, like intuition or insight, also suggests freedom, but it is the freedom from the constraints of rule-governed behavior and can be called freedom only until the control of the environment in evoking intuitive behavior is fully recognized.

The behavior of the scientist is often reconstructed by scientific methodologists within a logical framework of hypothesis, deduction, and the testing of theorems, but the reconstruction seldom represents the behavior of the scientist at work. Certain problems concerning the limitations of human knowledge might be closer to solution if the behavior of knowing were analyzed further. It has been said, for example, that science has reached a limit beyond which it cannot establish the determinacy of physical phenomena, and it has been argued that this may be the point at which freedom emerges in human behavior. Behavioral scientists would probably be quite content with the degree of rigor shown by physics in spite of this apparent limitation, but there may be something about the human organism which makes indeterminacy relatively important. We can discover whether or not that is an important limitation only by developing a science of human behavior to the point at which indeterminacy becomes apparent.

There would remain the possibility of investigating the behavior of the scientist and the nature of scientific knowledge to see whether some absolute limit has in fact been reached. Similar arguments have proved wrong in the past. For example, the limits of what could be seen through the microscope were once clearly established from a consideration of the wave lengths of visible light. Since then, of course, the electron microscope has proved that the earlier determination, though right on the evidence, was wrong with respect to the limits of microscopy.

16. It is not always clear what is meant when it is said that a behavioral analysis dehumanizes man or destroys man *qua* man. Sometimes the implication seems to be that its picture of man is incomplete: "Behaviorism tried to build a psychology without including man in his full complexity," or, "Behaviorism has omitted human phenomena which do not fit a physicalistic model." (Humanistic psychology, on the other hand, is said to be a science "appropriate to man as a subject matter," "committed to dealing with humanness in its own right," and "comprehensively human.") But phrases like "man *qua* man" or "man in his humanity" tell us very little about what has been left out.

Sometimes the implication is that behaviorism neglects something a person does because he is a member of the human species or keeps him from doing something he would otherwise do as such a member. The position of the French philosopher Georges Sorel has been paraphrased in this way:

Man, at his best, that is, at his most human, seeks to fulfill himself, individually and with those close to him, in spontaneous, unended, creative activity, in work that consists of the imposition of his personality on a recalcitrant environment. . . . He acts and is not acted upon, he chooses and is not chosen for. . . . He resists every force that seeks to reduce his energy, to rob him of his independence and his dignity, to kill the will, to

ABOUT BEHAVIORISM   238

crush everything in him that struggles for unique self-expression and reduce him to uniformity, impersonality, monotony, and, ultimately, extinction.

This characterization of the species is likely to be subscribed to by all those members of the species who can understand it, but it does not identify anything essentially human, as can be shown by applying it to another species. We can readily agree that a lion jumping through a hoop in a circus is not behaving *qua* lion, and we might elaborate in this way:

> The lion at his best, that is, at his most leonine, seeks to fulfill himself, individually and with those close to him, in spontaneous, unended, creative activity, in work that consists of the imposition of his leoninity on a recalcitrant environment. . . . He acts and is not acted upon. He chooses and is not chosen for. . . . He resists every force that seeks to reduce his energy, to rob him of his independence and his dignity, to kill the will, to crush everything in him that struggles for unique self-expression and reduces him to uniformity, unleoninity, monotony, and, ultimately, extinction.

I suspect that most lions would subscribe to this reassuring picture if they could.

It is often said that a behavioristic account somehow neglects something of what a person can be or do because it treats him as a machine. "Man comes to think of himself," as Martin Buber put it, "as if he were determined by the same mechanical laws that govern his refrigerator." But to assert that human behavior is lawful is not to say that the laws which govern it are as simple or as "mechanical" as those that apply to the operation of a refrigerator. Nor is the choice between (a) an entirely technological society in which persons are run by machines and (b) "an era of humanity with man at peace with himself by comporting with his natural environment." And we can scarcely deny that man *is* an animal, though a remarkable one. The complaint that Pavlov converted Hamlet's "How like a god!" into "How like a dog!" was answered by Hamlet himself: "In action how like an angel! In apprehension how like a god! The beauty of the world! The paragon of animals!" Man *is* the paragon of animals.

What is usually meant in saying that behaviorism dehumanizes man is that it neglects important capacities which are not to be found in machines or animals, such as the capacity to choose, have purposes, and behave creatively. But the behavior from which we infer choice, intention, and originality is within reach of a behavioral analysis, and it is not clear that it is wholly out of reach of other species. Man is perhaps unique in being a moral animal, but not in the sense that he possesses morality; he has constructed a social environment in which he behaves with respect to himself and others in moral ways.

Many of these issues were no doubt neglected in early versions of behaviorism, and methodological behaviorism systematically ruled some of them out of account, but I know of no essentially human feature that has been shown to be beyond the reach of a scientific analysis, and I doubt whether those who charge dehumanization would wish to rest their case on the inadequacy of a behavioral account, since the future might turn too heavily against them.

Behavior is the achievement of a person, and we seem to deprive the human organism of something which is his natural due when we point instead to the environmental sources of his behavior. We do not dehumanize him; we dehomunculize him. The essential issue is autonomy. Is man in control of his own destiny or is he not? The point is often made by arguing that a scientific analysis changes man from victor to victim. But man remains what he has always been, and his most conspicuous achievement has been the design and construction of a world which has freed him from constraints and vastly extended his range. No doubt he has been careless. In the nineteenth century man's overriding inhumanity to man came from the Industrial Revolution—the payment of wages to a hungry labor force, for example, neglected serious side effects. Marx is said to have described this under the influence of earlier romantic writers. Schiller, for example, had written: "Enjoyment was separated from labor, the means from the end, exertion from recompense. Eternally fettered only to a single little fragment of the whole, man fashions himself only as a fragment; ever hearing only the monotonous whirl of the wheel which he turns, he never displays the full harmony of his being." In other words, labor no longer had the reinforcing consequences which generate the condition felt as joy; the contingencies sustained a very narrow repertoire; a person had no chance to acquire most of the behavior of which he was capable.

Today other side effects are attracting more attention. Man continues to build machines which dehumanize him by dispensing with behaviors that contribute to his status as a person, but he is also breeding at a dangerous rate, exhausting the world's resources, polluting the environment, and doing little to relieve the threat of a nuclear holocaust. Nevertheless, if the position I have presented here is correct, he can remedy these mistakes and at the same time build a world in which he will feel freer than ever before and achieve greater things.

He can do this only if he recognizes himself for what he is. He has failed to solve his problems because he has looked in the wrong place for solutions. The extraordinary role of the environment opens the prospect of a much more successful future, in which he will be most human and humane, and in which he will manage himself skillfully because he will know himself accurately.

A science of behavior has been said to dehumanize man because it is reductionistic. It is said to deal with one kind of fact as if it were a different kind—as is done, for example, by physiological psychology. But behaviorism does not move from one dimensional system to another. It simply provides an alternative account of the same facts. It does not *reduce* feelings to bodily states; it simply argues that bodily states are and always have been what are felt. It does not *reduce* thought processes to behavior; it simply analyzes the behavior previously explained by the invention of thought processes. It does not *reduce* morality to certain features of the social environment; it simply insists that those features have always been responsible for moral behavior.

Even so, something in traditional formulations may seem to be missing. The problem is not peculiar to the behavioral sciences. Hold a slip of paper just above a candle flame and it will "catch fire." We speak of fire as something things catch and then possess. When we stop the burning, we are said to "put the fire out"; we "quench" it in the sense of causing it to vanish. The metaphor is probably harmless enough in casual discourse, but it is not particularly useful to the physicist, and a person who is accustomed to quenching fires by throwing water on them will be unhappy when he is told that water simply *cools* or *smothers* a fire. Cooling and smothering do not seem like quenching. But it would be wrong to say that the process of quenching had been "reduced" to cooling and smothering. The term has simply been translated into terms having a broader reference, and, as in similar instances in a behavioral analysis, what seems to be missing is nothing to be taken seriously, nor does it justify the charge of reductionism.

Behaviorism could perhaps be called reductionistic when it discusses the social sciences. It reduces social processes to the behavior of individuals. But that could scarcely be called a reduction of the role of the individual. It is, rather, a kind of aggrandizement.

17. Every science has probably been accused at one time or other of neglecting the uniqueness of the individual case

in its search for general principles. There is more in a sunset, a storm at sea, a blade of grass, or a piece of music than is dreamt of in philosophies or accounted for in science. Exposure to a unique contingency of reinforcement generates a special kind of knowing, and the feelings or introspectively observed states of mind associated with it differ widely from those produced when a person follows a rule or obeys a law. The specialist may come close to the unique event, but he never encompasses all of it.

Psychotherapy has naturally been concerned with the individual. Its stock in trade is the case history, with its endless fascination, and the intensive knowledge of another person acquired in therapeutic sessions is no doubt beyond the reach of a science which emphasizes generalities. Psychotherapy is largely responsible for the humanistic psychology which complains that behaviorism ignores the individual. As one may know the world in a sense quite different from knowing physical and biological science, so one may know *people* in a sense quite different from knowing behavioral science. It would be foolish to question the interest a person takes in others—in gossip, in autobiographies, in novels, in dramas, in news reports, and so on. Individuals are important parts of the environment, and although a science of behavior permits a person to interpret what he sees more effectively, it will never tell him the whole story about the individual case.

It is only when we ask what is to be done with knowledge that we begin to examine the different forms of knowing more closely and appreciate the value of the generality. Science must balance costs and gains, and though it may bear down hard on a unique event, especially in a technological application, it reaps a greater harvest from general principles.

18. Basic research in the science of behavior is essentially manipulative; the experimenter arranges conditions under which a subject behaves in a given way, and in doing so he

controls behavior. Because operant conditioning is conspicuous, it is often referred to as if it were nothing more than a technique to be used in the control of others. There is no doubt that it can be so used for nonscientific purposes and will be so used if the results are reinforcing. Among those who have the power needed to control others in this way are governmental and religious authorities and men possessing a good deal of money. We escape from them or attack their power when they resort to aversive methods or methods which have the deferred aversive consequences called exploitation. As we have seen, those who do not use their power in aversive or exploitative ways do not refrain because they possess compassion, or a sense of ethics, or a concern for the welfare of others, but because they have been subjected to countercontrol. Democracy is a version of countercontrol designed to solve the problem of manipulation.

The difference between conspicuous and inconspicuous control has led to many misunderstandings. It is sometimes said that children who are being *taught* verbal behavior are acquiring it through operant conditioning but that what they learn from a noninstructional verbal community is learned through some other process. Similarly, it has been said that government and economics are perhaps proper fields for a behavioristic analysis, but that art, literature, music, religion, and daily life are not. Children in a classroom organized on the principles of a token economy are felt to be controlled, but when it proves possible to abandon explicit reinforcement and to move on to such a natural reinforcer as successful accomplishment, the children are said to be free.

What is at issue is not the behavioral process but the contingencies. Contingencies designed for explicit purposes can be called manipulative, though it does not follow that they are exploitative; unarranged contingencies must be recognized as having equal power, and also possibly unhappy consequences. It must not be forgotten that exhortation, demagoguery, evangelism, and so on are also behavioral practices, as are similar practices on a smaller scale in daily life. We are all so used to being controlled to our disadvantage that to call a person harmless is to imply that he is totally ineffective or feeble-minded.

To say that all control is manipulative and hence wrong is to overlook important uses in education, psychotherapy, government, and elsewhere. A proposal to terminate behavioral research or to sequester its results on the grounds that they can be used by despots and tyrants would be a disastrous mistake, because it would undermine all the important contributions of the culture and interfere with the countercontrolling measures which keep aversive and exploitative control within bounds.

19. In an operant analysis of the stimulus control of verbal behavior, we can identify the referent of abstract terms, but terms like "morality" and "justice" raise an additional problem. It can be solved by recognizing that the behavior we call moral or just is a product of special kinds of social contingencies arranged by governments, religions, economic systems, and ethical groups. We need to analyze those contingencies if we are to build a world in which people behave morally and justly, and a first step in that direction is to dismiss morality and justice as personal possessions.

20. A common reaction to behaviorism runs as follows: "What you have said may all be true, but I am not interested in my behavior. I am interested in my feelings—and in the feelings of others. I read books because they intrigue or excite me; I listen to music because it exhilarates me; I look at pictures because I find them beautiful; I associate with people I love or with whom I enjoy talking about everyday things with everyday words." The same could be said, of course, about any science: "I do not care about immunology, I simply want to avoid disease"; "I do not care about genetics, I simply want healthy children"; "I do not care where energy

comes from, I simply want comfort and convenience." A knowledge of medicine, genetics, and technology does not interfere with feeling well, having healthy children, or being comfortable, and no one is likely to suppose that it does, but similar statements about behavior are debated. Yet there is nothing in a science of behavior or its philosophy which need alter feelings or introspective observations. The bodily states which are felt or observed are acknowledged, but there is an emphasis on the environmental conditions with which they are associated and an insistence that it is the conditions rather than the feelings which enable us to explain behavior.

Those who understand the theory or history of music do not find music therefore any less enjoyable, nor are those who understand the techniques of the artist or the history of art less likely to enjoy paintings. It is true that a touch of mystery may be reinforcing, and we may be particularly moved by the apparently inexplicable, but if there were no offsetting gains, educators would have a good deal to explain.

A distinguished critic of science has expressed an opposing view in the following way: ". . . according to [ethology] Keats is all wrong: the bird is not pouring forth its soul in ecstasy, for now we *know that all it is doing* is serving notice on its fellows that it claims a certain territory for worm grubbing." And he insists that we shall never know why birds sing, "but as poets we know—none better—how their singing affects us and as to this datum science has not a word to say; it can only listen too."

It seems to be implied that to understand why birds sing would interfere with the effect of their singing upon us, and upon the poet, and upon us when we read what he has to say. The ethologist would be wrong to take these effects into account in trying to discover why birds sing, but he can nevertheless enjoy bird song and also what a poet says about it. The bird sings not because of how it feels but because of certain contingencies of survival. How the poet feels upon hearing it is doubly irrelevant to why it sings, but there is no reason why the poet cannot tell us how he feels or, if he is a good poet, induce in us a condition felt in the same way.

If we stop to listen to a bird, it is because we are reinforced for doing so, and science can listen for other reasons. It can survey the extent to which sound patterns are or become reinforcing, and in doing so it may contribute to an explanation of why people compose and listen to music. The conditions generated within the body of the listener remain forever private, but the behavioral scientist may still investigate the reinforcing effects they are associated with and possibly discover how more reinforcing effects may be achieved.

Not only has the most ardent behaviorist feelings like everyone else; on balance he has quite possibly more enjoyable ones, because there are states of the body—associated, for example, with failure, frustration, or loss—which are far from enjoyable or reinforcing, and they are less likely to be experienced by those who practice scientific self-knowledge and self-management. And it is hard to see how a helpful interest in, or affection for, another person could be endangered by improved understanding.

THE BEHAVIORIST'S OWN BEHAVIOR

So much for the misunderstandings and criticisms listed in the Introduction. To them should perhaps be added the charge that the behaviorist constantly violates his own principles, most obviously by his continued use of mentalistic terms. He says, "I think"; he asks his readers to keep something "in mind"; he summarizes the "purport" or "purpose" of a passage; and so on. In the sample which the reader has now had a chance to examine, I believe I have been consistent in the following respects:

I have used technical terms in making a technical point. I have preferred a technical term elsewhere when it could be used at no great cost. Rather than say that our problem is "to create a concern for the future," I have preferred to say that it is "to induce people to act with respect to a future." I prefer the expression "It occurred to me . . ." to "The thought occurred to me." But elsewhere I have freely used the lay vocabulary while accepting the responsibility of providing a technical translation upon demand. There is no other way if a book of this kind is to be brief and readable. The reader who objects must also object to the physician who tells him that he has caught a "cold" (rather than a virus) or to the almanac which tells him when the sun will rise rather than when it will become visible over the horizon as the earth turns. The convenience of the lay vocabulary does not warrant its use where a technical alternative would be more helpful. Education, for example, has long suffered from efforts to analyze teaching and learning in lay terms.

The objection is not always a matter of vocabulary. Those who approach a behavioristic formulation for the first time may be surprised by the mention of self-control. Does this not suggest some kind of inner determination? Or happiness —does this not mean that feelings are important? The behaviorist's own behavior also seems to violate his principles. Has he not *decided* to write a book? Is he not clearly *responsible* for it, since it would not exist if he had not written it? Does he not *urge* his readers to adopt a behavioristic point of view? According to traditional definitions of self-control, happiness, decision, responsibility, and urging, the behaviorist is indeed inconsistent, but according to his own definitions he is not; and when the latter are understood, objections of this sort lose their force.

Another version takes this form: "If human behavior is as fully determined as the behaviorist says it is, why does he bother to write a book? Does he believe that anything matters?" To answer that question we should have to go into the history of the behaviorist. Nothing he says about human behavior seriously changes the effect of that history. His research has not altered his concern for his fellow men or his belief in the relevance of a science or technology of behavior. Similar questions might as well be asked of the author of a book on respiration: "If that is respiration, why do you go on breathing?"

ON THE POSITIVE SIDE

Behaviorism has so often been defined in terms of its supposed shortcomings—of what it is said to ignore or neglect—that setting the record straight often appears to destroy what was meant to be saved. In answering these charges I may seem to have "abandoned the very basis of behaviorism," but what I have abandoned are the vestiges of early statements of the position, subjected to various elaborations and criticisms over a period of some sixty years. What survives can be put in a positive form:

1. The position I have taken is based, as the reader was warned, on a particular kind of behavioral science. I have chosen it in part no doubt because of my familiarity with it but mainly because it has certain features especially relevant to the behavioristic argument. It offers, I believe, the clearest possible statement of the causal relations between behavior and environment. It analyzes individual data rather than group averages. The complexity of the experimental environment has gradually increased until it now approaches the complexity of daily life—in which, therefore, extrapolations from the laboratory become increasingly useful.

2. What we have learned from the experimental analysis of behavior suggests that the environment performs the functions previously assigned to feelings and introspectively observed inner states of the organism. This fact has been only slowly recognized. Only very strong evidence of the role of the environment could offset the effects of mentalism

in directing attention to supposed inner causes.

3. A behavioral analysis acknowledges the importance of physiological research. What an organism does will eventually be seen to be due to what it is, at the moment it behaves, and the physiologist will someday give us all the details. He will also tell us how it has arrived at that condition as a result of its previous exposure to the environment as a member of the species and as an individual.

4. A crucial step in the argument can then be taken: what is felt or seen through introspection is only a small and relatively unimportant part of what the physiologist will eventually discover. In particular it is not the system which mediates the relation between behavior and the environment revealed by an experimental analysis.

As the philosophy of a science of behavior, behaviorism calls for probably the most drastic change ever proposed in our way of thinking about man. It is almost literally a matter of turning the explanation of behavior inside out.

THE FUTURE OF BEHAVIORISM

A good deal of what is called behavioral science is not behavioristic in the present sense. Some of it, as we have seen, avoids theoretical issues by confining itself to the form, topography, or structure of behavior. Some of it appeals to the "conceptual nervous systems" of mathematical models and systems theories. Much of it remains frankly mentalistic. Perhaps this diversity is healthful: different approaches could be regarded as mutations, from which a truly effective behavioral science will eventually be selected. Nevertheless, the present condition is not promising. Even in a single part of the field it is unusual to find two authorities talking about precisely the same things, and although nothing could be more relevant to the problems of the world today, the actual accomplishments of behavioral science do not seem to be extensive. (It has been suggested that the science is "too young" to solve our problems. This is a curious example of developmentalism, in which immaturity offers a kind of exoneration. We forgive the baby for not walking because he is not yet old enough, and by analogy we forgive the asocial or disturbed adult because he has not quite grown up, but must we then wait until the behavioral sciences *grow* more effective?)

I contend that behavioral science has not made a greater contribution just because it is not very behavioristic. It has recently been pointed out that an International Congress on Peace was composed of statesmen, political scientists, historians, economists, physicists, biologists—and not a single behaviorist in the strict sense. Evidently behaviorism was regarded as useless. But we must ask what the conference achieved. It was composed of specialists from many different fields, who probably spoke the commonsense lingua franca of the layman, with its heavy load of references to inner causation. What might the conference have achieved if it could have abandoned this false scent? The currency of mentalism in discussions of human affairs may explain why conferences on peace are held with such monotonous regularity year after year.

To assert that a thoroughgoing behaviorism could make a great difference is almost inevitably to be asked: "Well, then, what do you suggest? What would *you* do about war, or population, or pollution, or racial discrimination, or the revolt of the young?" Unfortunately, to understand the principles involved in solving a problem is not to have the solution. To know aerodynamics is not at once to know how to design a plane, to know plate tectonics is not at once to know how to predict earthquakes, to understand the double helix is not at once to be able to create a new species. The details of a problem must be studied. Knowing the basic principles without knowing the details of a practical problem is no closer to a solution than knowing the details without knowing the basic principles. But problems can be solved, even the big ones, if those who are familiar with the details will also adopt a workable conception of human behavior.

When we say that science and technology have created more problems than they have solved, we mean physical and biological science and technology. It does not follow that a technology of behavior will mean further trouble. On the contrary, it may be just what is needed to salvage the other contributions. We cannot say that a science of behavior has failed, for it has scarcely been tried. And it will not be given a fair trial until its philosophy has been clearly understood. A distinguished social philosopher has said, "It is only through a change of consciousness that the world will be saved. Everyone must begin with himself." But no one can *begin* with himself; and if he could, it would certainly not be by changing his consciousness.

If it were true that "an ever greater danger than nuclear war arises from within man himself in the form of smouldering fears, contagious panics, primitive needs for cruel violence, and raging suicidal destructiveness," then we should be lost. Fortunately, the point of attack is more readily accessible. It is the environment which must be changed. A way of life which furthers the study of human behavior in its relation to that environment should be in the best possible position to solve its major problems. This is not jingoism, because the great problems are now global. In the behavioristic view, man can now control his own destiny because he knows what must be done and how to do it.

Bibliography

Although I have tried to cover the essentials of behaviorism as the philosophy of a science, I have not developed any issue as fully as the evidence would permit. Further details are, of course, to be found in an extensive literature of which, unfortunately, there is no good summary, and to which I shall not try to supply a key. The reader who may wish to go a little further, using the present terminology, may find a few topics discussed in other books of my own, to which references are abbreviated as follows:

SHB   Science and Human Behavior (New York: Macmillan, 1953)

VB   Verbal Behavior (New York: Appleton-Century-Crofts, 1957)

SR   Schedules of Reinforcement, with Charles B. Ferster (New York: Appleton-Century-Crofts, 1957)

TT   The Technology of Teaching (New York: Appleton-Century-Crofts, 1968)

COR   Contingencies of Reinforcement: A Theoretical Analysis (New York: Appleton-Century-Crofts, 1969)

BFD   Beyond Freedom and Dignity (New York: Alfred A. Knopf, 1971)

CR   Cumulative Record: A Selection of Papers, 3rd edn. (New York: Appleton-Century-Crofts, 1972)

SELECTED TOPICS

Behaviorism. Behaviorism at fifty, **COR**; **SHB**, Section I.

253

Introspection. The operational analysis of psychological terms, **CR**, Paper #25; **SHB**, Chapter 17; **VB**, pp. 130–46.

Innate endowment. The phylogeny and ontogeny of behavior, **COR**, Chapter 7.

Reflexes and conditioned reflexes. **SHB**, Chapter 4.

Operant behavior. **SHR**, Chapters 5–12.

Schedules of reinforcement. **SR**.

Verbal behavior. **VB**.

Thinking. **SHB**, Chapter 16.

Rule-governed behavior. An operant analysis of problem solving, **COR**, Chapter 6.

Creative behavior. **CR**, Papers #22 and #23.

The self. **SHB**, Chapter 17.

Self-management. **SHB**, Chapter 15.

Managing others. **SHB**, Chapter 20.

The problem of control. **SHB**, Sections V and VI; **CR**, Part I; **TT,** Chapter 9; Compassion and ethics in the care of the retardate, **CR**; **BFD**.

Inside the skin. The inside story, **COR**, Chapter 9.

SELECTED REFERENCES

Introduction
   John B. Watson: "Psychology as the Behaviorist Views It." *Psychological Review*, 1913, *20*, 158–77.
Chapter 2
   Walter D. Weimer: "On the Return of Plato: Psycholinguistics and Plato's Paradoxes of the *Meno.*" *American Psychologist,* January 1973.
Chapter 3
   Vannevar Bush, in *Fortune*, January 1965.
Chapter 4
   Arthur M. Wilson: *Diderot.* New York: Oxford University Press, 1972.

Chapter 5
W. C. Stebbins (ed.): *Animal Psychophysics*. New York: Appleton-Century-Crofts, 1970.
G. E. Stratton: *Theophrastus and the Greek Physiological Psychology Before Aristotle.* New York: Macmillan, 1917.

Chapter 7
The three cognitive psychologists: G. A. Miller, Eugene Galanter, and Karl Pribram. The announcement cited is reported on page 101 of *Beyond the Punitive Society*, Harvey Wheeler (ed.). San Francisco: W. H. Freeman, 1973.

Chapter 8
Cassirer, quoted by Arthur M. Wilson: *Diderot*.
Stendhal: *Journal* (entry for xxx avril 1810), Henry Debraye and Louis Royer (eds.). Paris, 1932.
Wilfred Sellars is credited by Weimer (reference under Chapter 2) with "the cryptic [sic] aphorism that with language, man's actions came to have reasons as well as causes."

Chapter 9
Michael Polanyi: *Personal Knowledge*. Chicago: University of Chicago Press, 1960.
P. W. Bridgman: *The Way Things Are*. Cambridge, Mass.: Harvard University Press, 1959.
Peter Gay: *The Enlightenment: An Interpretation*. Vol. II: *The Science of Freedom*. New York: Alfred A. Knopf, 1969.

Chapter 10
Hans-Hubert Schönzeler: *Bruckner*. London: Calder and Boyars, 1970.

Chapter 12
"Control as a passing phase." See William Leiss: *The Domination of Nature*. New York: Braziller, 1973.

Chapter 13
On physiological technology, see Leon R. Kass: "The New Biology: What Price Relieving Man's Estate?" *Science*, 1971, 174, 779–88.

Chapter 14
Karl R. Popper: *Of Clouds and Clocks*. St. Louis: Washington University Press, 1966.

Isiah Berlin (paraphrasing Sorel), in *Times Literary Supplement,* December 31, 1971.
On Marx and Schiller, see David McLellan: *Marx Before Marxism.* London: Macmillan, 1970.

Preparation of this book was supported by the National Institutes of Mental Health, Grant number K6-MH-21, 775-01.
I am indebted to Dr. Ernest Vargas and Dr. Julie Vargas for critical readings of the manuscript.

Index

i

A Note on the Type

The text of this book was set on the Linotype in a type face called Life. Brought out by the German type foundry of Ludwig and Mayer in 1964, Life is an adaptation by Francisco Simoncini of Times Roman, the popular British typeface. Designed especially for use in a newspaper, Times Roman is widely appreciated for its legibility. Life, with its angular points exaggerated to compensate for loss of detail in reproduction, seems ideally suited for both text and newspaper settings.

This book was composed at Cherry Hill Composition, Inc., Pennsauken, N.J., and printed and bound at Haddon Craftsmen, Scranton, Pa. The typography and binding design are by Christine Aulicino.